Training Wheels for
TEACHERS

What I Wish I'd Known My First 100 Days on the Job:
Wisdom, Tips, and Warnings from **EXPERIENCED TEACHERS**

EDITED BY RANDY HOWE

Kaplan Publishing
Published by Simon & Schuster, Inc.
1230 Avenue of the Americas
New York, NY 10020

For information regarding special discounts for bulk purchases, please contact Simon & Schuster Special Sales at 1-800-456-6798 or business@simonandschuster.com.

Kaplan ® is a registered trademark of Kaplan, Inc.

DESIGN: Lili Schwartz
COVER ILLUSTRATION: Kevin Ghiglione
EDITOR: Helena Santini

Manufactured in the United States of America

July 2004
10 9 8 7 6 5 4 3 2 1
Library of Congress Cataloging-in-Publication Data
ISBN: 0-7432-6152-6

TABLE OF CONTENTS

This book is dedicated to the students and staff of Putnam/Northern Westchester Board of Cooperative Educational Services as well as New Haven's MicroSociety Magnet School.

I would like to thank Helena Santini for her support and guidance. This could have been a book about endless discipline referrals and one too many budget requests denied. Instead, it is a grade made, a test passed, and a smile on a child's face. As it should be.

I would also like to thank Maureen McMahon for the opportunity to combine two of my loves into one meaningful project.

And finally, my gratitude and affection to Alicia and Noelle Solís. There is no sweeter procrastination than a visit from my girls!

ACKNOWLEDGEMENTS

Mark Twain once wrote that teaching is like trying to hold 35 corks underwater at once. On a daily basis, you are going to be asked to handle attendance, curriculum, grades, phone calls, doctor's notes, conferences, college recommendations, committee work, coaching, bus duty, shoe lace-tying and winter coat-zippering, professional development days, and graduate school at night.

In addition, you must answer to the administration, your fellow teachers, and most important, your students. (And don't forget the parents, who will go to great lengths for answers and insights—even popping up in the produce aisle while you're trying to shop!)

Student teaching and coursework may provide a hint of what's to come, but the second you set foot in your own classroom is the second the surprises begin. Not to worry, though. *Training Wheels for Teachers* will help you to survive, and even thrive, during your first hundred days on the job.

Packed with tips provided by our Voices of Experience—hundreds of skilled educators who have submitted their stories and advice—this book is a nuts-and-bolts look at the practical needs of teachers. The tales within these pages are sure to provide the support and advice that all "newbies" need.

The veteran teachers quoted here have happily offered their help so that you can be the best teacher possible; they have embraced the role of mentor so that you may someday do the same for another new teacher. **Let the learning continue.**

"It's like having a hundred balls thrown at you all at once and someone just says, "Catch!""

Fourth-grade teacher, New York, NY

Congratulations! You are about to make the world's most rewarding profession not just your job but your *career*. It is a lifelong journey like no other.

On the pages that follow, the Voices of Experience will weigh in on why they became teachers. More likely than not, you will hear some of your thoughts echoed in theirs. In turn, you will be given a heads-up as they discuss some of the surprises that come with the territory. Even though the dream of having a classroom of your own has finally come true, there are going to be difficult days. The best thing is to be prepared. So read on to find out just what those reasons for teaching are, and to learn about some of the challenges that await.

Why I Wanted to Be a Teacher

Teachers come by teaching in a number of ways and for a number of reasons. All that really matters is that they are working with kids; that they have chosen to give themselves to others. That being said, the quotes on the next few pages will tell you why our Voices of Experience chose the profession. In some cases, it seems the profession chose them!

My Family, My Childhood

My immigrant parents taught me how valuable education is, so I passionately desired to be a part of the educational system.

SPECIAL EDUCATION TEACHER, HARRISBURG, PA

Most every teacher I had made me feel safe and special. I knew that's what I wanted to be able to do for other kids. What better way to thank your own teachers than to pass down the best of what they gave you?

ENGLISH TEACHER, MIDDLEPORT, NY

My father and grandfather had been teachers, and I wanted to continue the family tradition.

SOCIAL STUDIES TEACHER, PITTSBURGH, PA

I didn't like high school, and it took me twenty years to get the nerve to enroll in college. I thought that if I could teach, my classroom would be a place where kids who were miserable at school might enjoy a different way of doing things.

GEOGRAPHY TEACHER, FOUKE, AR

I wanted to go into a profession that would help children who were struggling like I had once struggled.

SPECIAL EDUCATION TEACHER, LIMA, PERU

I was always very angry with the way most of my teachers taught. I wanted to run a classroom that respected all students, broke down stereotypes, and promoted all styles of learning.

FIFTH-GRADE TEACHER, BERLIN, CT

Doin' It for the Kids

So many students do not receive that "pat on the back" at home. Teachers can help show them that they count.

READING SPECIALIST, STATEN ISLAND, NY

I wanted to give students a role model. If I could accomplish anything that I wanted, so could they.

SCIENCE TEACHER, PACOIMA, CA

I became a teacher to help children in inner city schools strive for more than their surroundings.

MATHEMATICS TEACHER, CINCINNATI, OH

What job could possibly be more important in a democracy than working with young people to carry on our traditions?

ENGLISH TEACHER, JEFFERSON, ME

There is no greater honor or more distinguished duty than to be called to give one's self to the future.

SOCIAL STUDIES TEACHER, CHICAGO, IL

So Many Reasons to Teach

I love environmental science and wanted to infect other people with my enthusiasm. My neighbors wouldn't listen to me, so I had to find a captive audience!

ENVIRONMENTAL SCIENCE TEACHER, PATCHOGUE, NY

As I tell my students, if you know something and don't share it with anyone else, what good is knowing it?

COMPUTER SCIENCE TEACHER, FOUNTAIN, CO

I love the idea of continuously learning.

ENGLISH TEACHER, SILVERDALE, WA

I am almost fifty-seven years old and find I am younger because of what I do.

THIRD-GRADE TEACHER, CHULA VISTA, CA

I was working in the business world and found that unchallenging. I'm happier now and feel my being in the classroom makes a difference in the lives of my students.

FIFTH-GRADE TEACHER, HOPEWELL JUNCTION, NY

The Real Deal

Now that you're feeling all warm and fuzzy, it's time to get down to the nitty-gritty! The previous section is a reminder as to why we all signed up in the first place, but over the next few pages the Voices of Experience will describe the realities you will most likely face over your first hundred days. Hopefully, after reading through this book, you won't be quite so shocked the first time a student lies to your face, a plan falls flat on its face, or you face a tab of $50 for supplies.

So many demands are put on you that most days your head will end up spinning like a propeller! Just remember, what goes up must come down, and you *will* land on both feet.

Can You Say, "Whirlwind"?

It was much more "seat of the pants" and a lot less planned than I anticipated.

LIFE SKILLS TEACHER, LOWELL, MA

In one day's time I went from having no children (I wasn't even married yet) to having twenty-eight!

SECOND-GRADE TEACHER, NEW HAVEN, CT

You quickly learn that you never have a free moment, from the time you walk into the building until the time you leave.

COMPUTER TEACHER, JOLIET, IL

Be prepared to go well beyond the "contract day."

SOCIAL STUDIES TEACHER, CHEHALIS, WA

"**I was shocked that professional adults could not use the bathroom whenever they wanted and that they would fight over the copier.**

FOURTH-GRADE TEACHER, CHANDLER, AZ

My legs hurt from standing up all day; five classes at 45 minutes each. On the other hand, I realized just how many lives I could affect every single day.

WORLD STUDIES TEACHER, CHICAGO, IL

I did not expect all of the details, details, details: the routines of daily life in a school and the "hidden curriculum" concerning everything from when you take your students to lunch to how to respond to the many memos you receive from the administration.

SIXTH-GRADE TEACHER, PRICE, UT

Time Is a Scarce Resource

Everything took longer than expected. Lessons took longer to teach than planned. Planning and preparation took longer than the planning period. It often took many tries to contact parents. And it took longer than I thought it would for me to feel comfortable in my role as teacher.

FOURTH-GRADE TEACHER, FRESNO, CA

Grading papers was much more time-consuming than I imagined.

SPANISH TEACHER, BALTIMORE, MD

The scheduling blew my mind. I had no idea you had to work around everyone else's schedule. Kids are pulled out for music, art, gym, and library. It's a real juggling act.

FOURTH-GRADE TEACHER, BARTOW, FL

Learning to multitask took a while. Managing my time better has been good for me personally and professionally.

LANGUAGE ARTS TEACHER, BEACHWOOD, OH

13

Working with Adults

I did not anticipate so much pressure from the administration. Sometimes it seemed like the principal was at my desk more than my students!

MATHEMATICS TEACHER, BALTIMORE, MD

I thought I'd have to fight to get the parents involved. The real fight was getting them involved in a positive way.

KINDERGARTEN TEACHER, TALLAHASSEE, FL

I could not believe how many teachers walked into the classroom during my tests and spoke in a loud voice.

SPANISH TEACHER, NEWTON, MA

Money, Money, Money

Students are suffering because of all the budget cuts. Extra time and teacher creativity is required to make and develop materials.

SPECIAL EDUCATION TEACHER, NATOMA, KS

The teacher I replaced took everything! Aside from a few torn-apart teacher manuals, I had no supplies.

SCIENCE TEACHER, ALPENA, MI

I thought the school district would have teacher supplies or at least help defray the cost of buying supplies. Untrue. I organized my classroom and paid for everything on my walls, bulletin boards, and doors.

MATHEMATICS TEACHER, NORTH CHICAGO, IL

I thought the district would be able to provide me with a scope and sequence for the grade level and subjects I was teaching as well as a textbook for each student. Not so; there had been severe budget cuts the year before.

MATHEMATICS TEACHER, SAN FRANCISCO, CA

15

Where Expectations Meet Reality

I thought since I was teaching freshman English in an affluent suburb, my students would be well versed. I discovered that their writing skills were extremely weak. All of the jazzed-up lessons I'd planned over the summer had to be set aside so that we could review the basics.

LANGUAGE ARTS TEACHER, NEWARK, NJ

When I switched careers to the classroom, I had to slow down. Students work at a much slower pace than people in the business world.

COMPUTER SCIENCE TEACHER, TAMPA, FL

During my first one hundred days as a teacher I did a lot more organizing and disciplining than teaching.

THIRD-GRADE TEACHER, PEARL CITY, IL

I had no idea that there were so many "standards" to prepare for. I didn't realize that there were specific skills to be mastered at each grade level and that I was responsible for making sure they were covered. I dealt with it by taking all the curriculum guides home and becoming a student again.

SECOND-GRADE TEACHER, WOODRIDGE, IL

I thought I would get rapt attention. Instead, I was ignored.

LANGUAGE ARTS TEACHER, PATCHOGUE, NY

I was surprised by the way cliques spill over into the classroom dynamic. It took a lot of human relations work to help students respect each other and get beyond some of the petty divisions that they use to separate themselves.

CHARACTER EDUCATION TEACHER, CHICAGO, IL

Flying Solo

I thought that other teachers would be helpful, but I basically had to sink or swim.

FIRST-GRADE TEACHER, PITTSBURGH, PA

It was more isolating than I thought. You are given the curriculum, books, students, a room, and then let go. They expect you to hit the ground running.

KINDERGARTEN TEACHER, BALTIMORE, MD

Connecting with Kids

I did not expect the widespread apathy from so many students. It is very difficult to teach them when they don't consider their education to be important.

MATHEMATICS TEACHER, STATEN ISLAND, NY

Children are so much more complex than educational theory implies. There are constant questions, comments, complaints, observations, and random noises. Some days it's like herding a swarm of mosquitoes.

FIFTH-GRADE TEACHER, EAST AURORA, NY

Even though I knew I'd chosen a "caring" profession, I didn't expect to be placed so often in the role of parent, counselor, and advisor. The issues students have brought to me over the years seem to be growing, not only in number but in severity and importance.

JOURNALISM TEACHER, SUMMERTON, SC

"I was more exhausted than I ever thought I'd be, but also more emotionally invested in my students than I had anticipated.

FIRST-GRADE TEACHER, DAVIS, CA

I was surprised by how quickly I learned about my students. It didn't take long to understand their personalities and academic strengths and weaknesses.

FIFTH-GRADE TEACHER, DALLAS, TX

Many of the students I work with really craved attention, love, empathy, and compassion much more than an academic lesson.

SPECIAL EDUCATION TEACHER, INDIANAPOLIS, IN

The Traits All Good Teachers Share

Clearly the last few pages have shown that teachers need to be ready to deal with a multitude of issues. Are you ready? Will you be able to rise to the occasion? Of course! But just as a reminder, here are six characteristics that all good teachers share:

- Strong interpersonal skills, including patience, compassion, and objectivity
- Good listening skills
- Enthusiasm for, and dedication to, your students and subject matter
- A pervasively positive, benevolent attitude
- Self-control in matters ranging from discipline to prioritizing
- Professional and personal goals

teacher tip Although some teachers will say that if you don't love teaching, you should find a different job, our Voices of Experience beg to differ. Give yourself time to adjust; find things you can work on to better enjoy your job . . . and work on them the best you can!

Surprises come with the territory, as does stress. You'll want to make minimizing stress one of your priorities. This won't be easy—especially on day one! But in the next chapter you'll find that the Voices of Experience have some suggestions on things you should do even *before* the first day of school to help keep the blood pressure down and the corners of your lips up!

Just remember: those 35 corks don't swim so much as bob. The important thing is knowing that they won't sink. And neither will you.

2

Starting Off on the Right Foot

> "Don't feel like you have to conform to a "norm" of teaching. There are no norms!
>
> *Third-grade teacher, Pearl City, IL*

Before you meet your principal, before you arrange the students' desks, before you plan that first lesson, you must find a school that's a good fit for *you*. Doing so can mean the difference between a positive and a not-so-positive teaching experience.

After you've found a job, get ready to do some legwork. Have you thought of what needs to be done between now and the first day? The folks you should talk to? The materials you should gather? The systems you should plan out? What kind of first impression you want to make on students and colleagues? In this chapter, the Voices of Experience will take you from interviewing through day one. There's much to be done before the first bell rings!

Getting the Job

Okay, first thing's first. You have to get a job. But even more, you have to get the *right* job. During your interview, be sure to slip in the following questions. That way, you'll show just how insightful you are while also getting a greater sense of the school!

■ What is the first professional development opportunity offered to new teachers?

■ What additional duties outside the classroom are expected of teachers?

■ When can I expect to meet my mentor?

■ What is the top schoolwide priority going into this year?

■ Is there one book, movie, quote, or motto that best reflects the culture of this school?

■ Where's the nearest Dunkin' Donuts?

Time to Do Your Homework!

Collect data about the town. Ask everyone from real estate agents to cashiers about what families do for fun, what kind of community outreach is available, if arts and athletics are important, and if teenagers are more likely to have a job, a car, or both; anything to clue you in on your new environment.

SCIENCE TEACHER, SAN JUAN, PUERTO RICO

I would say the best thing to do is become culturally aware: of the department culture, the school culture, the community culture(s). . . . You will be able to connect better with your students and colleagues if you know what to expect ahead of time.

WORLD LANGUAGES TEACHER, MAYFIELD, NY

Know exactly what you are getting yourself into by asking quality questions. You are interviewing them as much as they are interviewing you!

ORCHESTRA TEACHER, GILLETTE, WY

If You're Still Student Teaching . . .

Student teach a full day of classes including all the prep work, grading, and everything that goes with it. Take on a few extracurricular duties and even volunteer for a committee or two. This will provide the best representation of what a teacher's day is like. **HISTORY TEACHER, LAFAYETTE, LA**

Ask for help from anyone who is willing to help. **FRENCH TEACHER, ACCORD, NY**

I believe that every new teacher should have a year of substituting or interning before taking on a class of his or her own. Once you are the teacher, a lot of the supports you previously enjoyed in school are removed, and the more experience you have without those supports, the better prepared you will be.

THIRD-GRADE TEACHER, CHASKA, MN

It is important to read books for educators *by* educators. **HISTORY TEACHER, BROOKLYN, NY**

Before the First Day

Congratulations! You aced the interview, you've been hired for your first job, and now you're ready for the school year to begin. Or are you? There are many steps you should take to prepare in advance. For example:

■ **Once you have access to your school, take advantage.** Get to know the building, especially the physical layout. (How can you direct your students through a fire drill if you don't know where hallway B and concourse 2 are?)

■ **Speak to a building steward (your union representative) regarding union requirements.** What will be deducted from your paycheck for union dues (even if you decide not to participate)? How can you obtain a copy of the most up-to-date union contract?

Starting Off on the Right Foot

■ **Ask the principal what is expected of you before school starts.** Is there a handbook you should read, standards to memorize, a curriculum you must follow? Chances are, the answer is "Yes" to all three!

■ **Meet as many teachers in the building as you can.** Not only will they be able to give you helpful tips about the inner workings of the school, you'll have made some new friends you can go to for help during those first crazier-than-you-can-imagine hundred days.

teacher tip If you are superbusy, you can talk to your union rep once the school year begins. If you do wait, bring along your paycheck so that everything, especially the union deductions, can be explained to you.

Planning Your Routines

Plan out all of your routines: how the students will sit, line up, unpack, take out materials, and gain your attention. Plan when they will be allowed to go to the bathroom or get water and how they should make those requests.

KINDERGARTEN TEACHER, NEW YORK, NY

Make sure you have your routines clearly established. If children know what to expect in terms of where materials are located, what time they will go to lunch, and what you expect from them, it will make your day go much more smoothly.

SPECIAL EDUCATION TEACHER, SPRINGFIELD, VA

Be flexible in plans, be prepared for the inevitable, and go with the flow. Being too rigid only frustrates you and impacts your performance in the classroom.

FIFTH-GRADE TEACHER, GREECE, NY

You Can't Wing Classroom Management

We'll discuss discipline more in chapter 4, but the Voices of Experience wanted to emphasize that your behavior plan (rules, consequences, etc.) is definitely something you should have established *before* you find yourself in a discipline situation:

Have a behavior plan in mind and stick to it. What are your expectations? What are your consequences? If you don't know, they won't know.

SPECIAL EDUCATION TEACHER, NORFOLK, VA

I set high expectations for the students and have a clear plan for working toward that goal. A large part of my responsibility is putting a stop to anything that disrupts learning time.

THIRD-GRADE TEACHER, INDIANOLA, MI

Run your discipline plan by the principal. Make sure she is in agreement and will support your decisions. You also want to make sure you aren't opening yourself up to legal repercussions.

SEVENTH- AND EIGHTH-GRADE MATH TEACHER, WABAN, MA

New teachers need to know who is near their room in case of an "extreme" situation. It's nice to know that they can send a student over to Teacher X for a time out, if necessary.

PHYSICS TEACHER, LAREDO, TX

Setting Up the Classroom: What Goes Where?

The most important thing that should be done before the first day of school is setting up your classroom. Here are some questions you should ask yourself; answering them will definitely help you make some of the layout decisions.

■ **What style will you use for the majority of your lessons?**

Whole group? Small group? Independent? If you will use all three (which is recommended by the Voices of Experience) then arrange the desks so that it will be easy for the students to move them on command.

■ **How can I make some of this space my own?**

Find a spot for a framed photo or two on your desk or buy a desk lamp for when students are out of the room (soothing lighting is a necessity!).

■ **Along which wall are the Internet connections?**

This will impact where you put your computer tables as well as your own desk (hopefully you will have a few computers in your room).

★ THE FACT OF THE MATTER ★

In 2000, only 80 percent of schools had broadband Internet access.

In 2002, that number increased to an incredible 94 percent. In addition, between home and school, nine out of ten school-age children (6 to 17 years old) have access to a computer.

Source: "Inside the Stats!" U.S. Department of Education. 2004. nces.ed.gov.
Source: "9-in-10 School-Age Children Have Computer Access; Internet Use Pervasive, Census Bureau Reports." United States Census Bureau. 2001.
www.census.gov/Press-Release/www/2001/cb01-147.html.

The Layout of Your Room

Get into the classroom as early and as often as possible before the school year begins. It will take longer to set up than you anticipate.

FIFTH-GRADE TEACHER, MONTPELIER, VT

I don't keep the same layout for more than a month, because some students figure out ways to "hide" in it. Every once in a while, move the kids in back up to the front and vice versa.

SCIENCE TEACHER, PACOIMA, CA

Be it a piñata hanging from the ceiling or the desks arranged in a circle, some units require a complete change in the room. Doing so helps in ways big and small. It sets the tone and allows the kids to really get into the subject matter.

SECOND-GRADE TEACHER, SCITUATE, MA

The Students' Desks

"I use a pretty traditional row arrangement for my students' desks (6 x 6). I love the U-shape—it helps conversation—but the room I'm in now doesn't permit it.

LANGUAGE ARTS TEACHER, SANDY, UT

I arrange the student desks in pods of four, which is conducive to cooperative learning.

STAFF DEVELOPER, FARMINGTON, ME

It is better to start the year with the desks in groups of two and then put them into larger groups sometime around November. I always use heterogeneous grouping (pairing more advanced students with less advanced students) so that students can help one another.

FIFTH-GRADE TEACHER, BERLIN, CT

I keep my desks in traditional rows but often have students rearrange them into small groups. This breaks the monotony of the period and gives the students the chance to move about.

SOCIAL STUDIES TEACHER, YORKTOWN HEIGHTS, NY

Your Desk

I have my desk in the opposite corner from the door. This makes it possible for students to get to their desks without having to pass through my space. It also helps them to claim more ownership of the classroom.

FRENCH TEACHER, CHARLOTTESVILLE, VA

Studies show that the best place for the teacher's desk is in the back of the room. This allows for easy observation when independent work or testing is taking place. This also opens up space in the front of the classroom, where most activity occurs.

ENGLISH TEACHER, ANAHEIM, CA

I place my desk near the door with my back against the wall so that I can always see who is coming and going and am near the door if I need to get help.

SPECIAL EDUCATION TEACHER, BALTIMORE, MD

Fun with Furniture

I have a table with the day's activities placed in baskets for each subject. Ongoing assignments are also held in these baskets until the due date.

ENGLISH TEACHER, SAN DIEGO, CA

I keep a small podium in the front of the room, and it offers some security to children who are speaking in front of the class.

FIRST-GRADE TEACHER, OSCEOLA, WI

Even though I teach math, when kids finish their work, they can go to my bookshelf for something to read. Some of the books are even nonfiction, in case the student is interested in factual information rather than fiction.

PRE-ALGEBRA TEACHER, SENOIA, GA

Decorating Your Classroom

Teaching is an art, and never is this more obvious than in the way a classroom is decorated. Although most of the wall space should be reserved for student work, a teacher's style always finds ways to shine through: around the chalkboard, hanging from the ceiling, everywhere!

The following checklist offers some predecorating advice:

■ **Ask your colleagues where you can find supplies or catalogs for materials.** You will want to order many things for your classroom; if there aren't any catalogs in the staff lounge, ask around to find out where they are hidden. Also, make sure you know where materials are located within the school or you might wind up knee-deep in paint when you realize you have no idea where the stepladder is!

■ **Check the rules with the principal and custodian.** What percentage of the walls and ceiling are you allowed to cover with decorations? Are you allowed to paint your classroom walls? Are there any subsequent rules on painting?

39

■ **Seek out hand-me-downs.** Do the other teachers have some grade- or subject-specific decorations you can use?

■ **Find reimbursement opportunities.** This really varies from school to school, but ask if there is anything in the budget for all of those small items you'll purchase throughout the year. Even if it's just $50 in June, every little bit helps, and remember: you can write off $250 in school supplies on your tax return.

★ THE FACT OF THE MATTER ★

On average, teachers spend $443 on student supplies and other such educational materials.
An astounding 8 percent reported spending more than $1,000 per year!

Source: "Status of the American Public School Teacher: 2000–2001." National Education Association. 2003. http://www.nea.org/edstats/images/status.pdf.

Up on the Walls

I use bulletin board space for student work so as to make the room *our* learning community rather than *my* room in which they spend their days.

STAFF DEVELOPER, FARMINGTON, ME

During the summer I painted the peeling blue wallpaper in my classroom a bright white. It opened up the classroom and made it feel larger, brighter, and happier.

SPECIAL EDUCATION TEACHER, INDIANAPOLIS, IN

Across the front wall of the room, we have our rules, consequences, class creed (pledge), and class vision (goals for the year); the last two we say together every morning.

THIRD-GRADE TEACHER, INDIANOLA, MI

"

If it won't help in some way, don't put it up on the wall; cute is not enough.

FIRST-GRADE TEACHER, MONTGOMERY VILLAGE, MD

Decorations are mainly resource materials for shapes, colors, the alphabet, numbers; student work is posted at the room entrance for all to see. The fire marshal forbids more than 20 percent of the walls to be covered with anything flammable.

KINDERGARTEN TEACHER, BRADENTON, FL

I always try to create an even balance of my materials and student work on the wall. It's not as easy as it sounds—you often find you have more things to hang than there is room.

THIRD-GRADE TEACHER, UNIONDALE, NY

I found most of what I needed at dollar stores, flea markets, and the Salvation Army. It's good to be cost-conscious!

FOURTH-GRADE TEACHER, BROOKSVILLE, FL

I must have spent over a thousand dollars on decorations and supplies. And I forgot to keep receipts! I was just so excited, but I should have limited my expenses.

SCIENCE TEACHER, LOUISVILLE, KY

For All You Floaters

What if you will be sharing your classroom for the rest of the year? Or worse yet, what if you don't *have* a classroom, and each period of the day you will have to roll a cart from one side of the building to the other, chasing your students down like a border collie herds sheep? It could happen. Resources are more limited than ever. Prepare . . . to share.

I dealt with the pylons and floor hockey sticks, and the gym teacher dealt with my white board and alphabet carpet squares. Once, we even combined lessons. It actually worked out quite nicely, being able to use the gym as a resource room!

SPECIAL EDUCATION TEACHER, HOUSTON, TX

If you resign yourself to making the best of a bad situation, like three teachers using one room over the course of the day, you will be just fine.

ELEMENTARY MUSIC TEACHER, ATLANTA, GA

The best thing I ever did was put my rolling suitcase to work. It saved me hours at the chiropractor!

SPANISH TEACHER, EASTON, CT

Sharing multiple classrooms was an unexpected problem. I tried to set an example by having my students keep the rooms as clean as possible so that other teachers would do the same.

GLOBAL STUDIES TEACHER, CHICAGO, IL

The August Letter

Once you have everything set up and ready to go, you will want to welcome both students and parents to your classroom. Two weeks before classes start, send home a letter that details the following:

■ How much you're looking forward to meeting the students and to working with them (and their parents!) during the upcoming school year

■ A little bit about yourself and a little bit about what will be taught that year

■ Your email address, in case parents have questions before the first day and throughout the year (this will save you *hours* on the phone)

■ A subtle reminder of when the first day of school is

Remember, the tone of this letter should be cheerful; its purpose is to get everyone in the right frame of mind for the first day of school.

teacher tip Check with your principal to see if there is a standard letter the school wants sent out before you send your own. You may be able to use both or will find that sending your own would be repetitive after sending the school's.

Tomorrow, It All Begins

The night before that first day of school . . . relax. Sleep as best you can. You want to start off on the right foot, but worrying about what still needs to be done shouldn't interfere with your rest. The school year is a marathon and not a sprint; there's always more to do. But don't worry. Whatever you didn't get to yet, you have another 180-plus days to make amends!

> Don't do a thing the night before your first day of school. Go see a movie. Have a glass of wine. Play some tennis. Nothing you can do now will make the first day any easier!
>
> **CHEMISTRY TEACHER, DALLAS, TX**

> **Freeze a month's worth of dinners, because your evenings will be spent lesson planning and organizing your materials for the next day.**
>
> **THIRD- AND FIFTH-GRADE TEACHER, BROOKLYN, NY**

> Practice bladder control!
>
> **LANGUAGE ARTS TEACHER, NEWARK, NJ**

48

Day One

If one thing's for sure, it's that you'll be dispensing a large amount of information in a short period of time on the first day of school. Whether you're teaching older or younger students, don't forget to tell them how much you're going to enjoy being their teacher! Here are a few more things that you should be sure to do on the first day:

- **Dress professionally.** You only get one shot at a first impression.
- **Greet your students at the door and seat them alphabetically.** This will help you memorize their names (the students will be very impressed the first time you call them by name) and keep chatty friends apart.
- **Introduce yourself and make clear your expectations.** Make sure you cover both behavioral and academic expectations. Answer clarifying questions if necessary.
- **Teach hand signals** for "bathroom" and "water"—this will minimize interruptions during your lessons.

■ **Conduct a short icebreaker** that allows the students to get to know one another—and you! Try a "Pair and Share" where partners interview each other and then report back to the class on what they've learned.

■ **Hand out all school forms.** Cover all emergency procedures.

■ **Introduce your grading system.** Explain how you weigh assignments and class participation (more to follow on this in chapter 3).

■ **After school, remember to ask colleagues how their day went.** Don't just talk about yourself. The first day is hectic for everyone, veterans included!

teacher tip From this day forward, be a rampant hand washer! The younger the students, the more you'll want to wash. There is many a germ to be found in your school.

So Much to Remember . . .

Be overprepared, but don't expect to complete all the tasks you set out to accomplish. There's always tomorrow.

SPECIAL EDUCATION TEACHER, PITTSBURGH, PA

The first day is a blur. Establish yourself as friendly but not to be fooled with. Give a "getting to know you" homework assignment and quiz them the second day on something important you said during the first day.

GLOBAL STUDIES TEACHER, BEDFORD, NY

Remember to breathe, to eat lunch, to praise at least one student, and to allow yourself some sort of reflection (a conversation, an email summarizing the day, something!) after it's all over.

ENGLISH TEACHER, ST. LOUIS, MO

51

If you think it's hard to get organized before school starts . . . just wait till school begins! There will be meetings, papers to correct, and planning galore, and you *will* feel overwhelmed. Never fear. The next chapter will help you steer clear of disorganization.

3

Planning, Paperwork, and Prioritizing

"
It's not the hours you put into your work, but the work you put into your hours.

Fifth-grade teacher, Berlin, CT

"

When dealing with the amount of planning and paperwork that teachers face on a daily basis, it's oh so important to know how to prioritize. As much as this requires your time, it also requires your common sense. To avoid burnout, a newbie must know how to set limits. Sacrificing your life outside of school may mean, in the end, sacrificing your life as an educator. And none of us want that! Start with rule number one: Rest on Sundays. For some more helpful tips on organizing your life at school, start reading this chapter!

Lesson Planning

Lesson planning can be one of the biggest time drains for teachers. Depending on your district, you may find yourself spending hours on lesson plans long after the school day has ended. As you would expect, plans may vary from grade to grade and subject to subject, but there are a few steps that all teachers should take *before* they begin to plan:

STEP ONE: Digest the school curriculum. Massive tomes filled with teaching standards loom large on shelves in department offices and staff lounges. Flip through and absorb what the district and state have prescribed, incorporating as much as possible into your plans. Most principals are now asking for standards to appear within your plans, so find out the specifics for your school.

STEP TWO: Find out if your principal wants your lesson plan set up in a particular manner. Usually, teachers are asked to leave their lesson plans out every two weeks for an administrator to review while casually observing your class. Some principals are more specific than others in their requests.

STEP THREE: Ask other teachers if you can take a look at their lesson plans for ideas.

Offer to show them yours, too!

STEP FOUR: Choose a method for judging student progress and incorporate it into your lesson. Here are

some examples of different methods; more likely than not, you will end up using them all.

■ **Benchmarks:** district- or state-generated tests, given on fixed dates throughout the year.

■ **Quizzes and tests:** teacher-generated assessments that can range from verbal Q&A to essays.

■ **Rubrics:** graphs that lay out the methods for testing as well as *how* the students will be assessed.

STEP FIVE: Decide how you will create your lesson plans. Will you do your planning on the computer? Or will

you write in a plan book? The Voices of Experience weigh in on the pros of each later in the chapter.

Surfing for Ideas

Now that you know the basics, it's time to start fleshing out your ideas for your lesson plans. An excellent source of inspiration is the Internet! Here are some websites that might be of help:

www.education-world.com

www.edsitement.neh.gov

www.teachers.net/lessons

www.thirteen.org/edonline/lessons

www.teachnet.com

www.school.discovery.com/lessonplans

www.theteacherscorner.net

www.coollessons.org

www.lessonplansearch.com

www.moteachingjobs.com/lessons/mainsearch.cfm

Putting Technology to Use

Saving your lesson plan outline as a template on the computer is a real time saver. Instead of rewriting the whole thing, you just fill in the blanks from day to day.

SPECIAL EDUCATION TEACHER, MERRILLVILLE, IN

I set up a table in Microsoft Word for my lesson plans. If my class doesn't finish something one week, I just cut and paste the plan into the next week's lesson.

THIRD-GRADE TEACHER, MODESTO, CA

I am most comfortable with having books and a pad in front of me, so I write my lessons out. And I promise: I *am* someone who is computer literate!

SECOND-GRADE TEACHER, ROCHESTER, NY

Remember Your Audience

When writing your lesson plans, ask yourself, "What do I want the students to learn? How will they learn it?" Include objectives, procedures, and methods of assessment in your plans and make them relevant to the students' interests.

FOURTH- AND FIFTH-GRADE TEACHER, COLUMBUS, OH

The more a lesson can appeal to different types of learners, the more successful your students will be. One size or style of teaching does not fit all.

SPECIAL EDUCATION TEACHER, ORLANDO, FL

Consider your plans from the students' viewpoint: What will be engaging? What will be enjoyable? What are the difficult parts? Why are we doing this activity?

FIFTH-GRADE TEACHER, EAST AURORA, NY

Know your content, know your state's standards, and know the ins and outs of child development. Be prepared with multiple learning styles and differentiated teaching strategies.

HISTORY TEACHER, CHARLESTON, SC

The Big Picture

Plan one unit at a time. See the whole picture, outline it, and then break it down into smaller lessons.

HEBREW TEACHER, LIVINGSTON, NJ

Before you start planning, block out days off, assemblies, etc. This way you will know that instead of 20 days, a unit will take 24 because of interruptions.

LANGUAGE ARTS TEACHER, SANDY, UT

Use your lesson plans to reflect on how the lesson went and to make the appropriate changes for the next lesson.

KINDERGARTEN TEACHER, DETROIT, MI

Making the Grade

Another aspect of teaching that takes up a lot of time is grading—and this is a topic that students are especially interested in! You'll have to tell them right off the bat what your grading system is . . . and then stick with it. But how do you know where to begin?

A general rule that works for many teachers is to divide the grading system into three sections: Effort (everything from being on time to class participation), Quizzes and Tests, and Assignments and Projects. This tends to work well if you weigh each section equally, but like the recipe says, "Season to taste!" After completing a general outline for the quarter, you will know how many assignments, quizzes, or projects you'll be giving and will be better able to determine how much each subsection will be worth in the student's overall grade.

teacher tip — Some teachers set the bar high at the beginning of the year by grading a little tougher than they normally would. Just as many students will underachieve if they think you are a soft grader, they will work hard to meet your expectations if those expectations are high.

Get Your Grading Under Control

There are many variables when it comes to constructing and correcting assignments, and the approach you choose can mean the difference between an hour of grading and five hours of grading. Here are some hints from the Voices of Experience on how to get the most out of your assignments while retaining most of your time:

■ Multiple choice is less time-consuming to grade than short answer.

■ Students are capable of checking their own work, as well as each other's.

■ Not every assignment needs to be graded; sometimes verbally assessing comprehension is enough.

■ Grading reports and projects should be as objective as possible, so cover the students' names.

■ Make sure you are well rested and relatively cheerful while grading. You don't want your mood to be reflected in your students' grades.

■ If you say you're going to grade the work, be sure to do it. Your students will be looking forward to the feedback.

■ Returning graded assignments on time sets a good example.

■ Also, returning them as soon as possible keeps your pile from waxing and their enthusiasm from waning.

Standards and Evaluation

I was overwhelmed by the amount of grading I was doing. I reviewed every single piece of homework, class work, every quiz and test. I forced myself to start picking and choosing what I would grade.

MATHEMATICS TEACHER, HANAU, GERMANY

Understanding the scope and sequence of the curriculum means you will know what the students are expected to know. Only with this information will you be able to grade appropriately.

SCIENCE AND SOCIAL STUDIES TEACHER, WESLACO, TX

I gave a grade that was too high because I believed it would build confidence. My plan backfired. The student knew the paper and the grade were garbage, and he lost respect for me because I expected so little of him.

ENGLISH TEACHER, PORT ORCHARD, WA

Rubrics are a fantastic tool for outlining expectations and scoring, as well as making sure that you cater to the needs of all your students. They are most useful when you let students grade themselves.

SEVENTH-GRADE TEACHER, PORT AUGUSTA, AUSTRALIA

Forms and Other Paperwork

Lesson plans, tests, assignments, report cards—these are only a few examples of all that you will be asked to fill out and file. Here are some others you should be aware of:

■ **The School Improvement Plan:** This is a plan that allows the superintendent to know what each of the district's schools is doing to address the standards as well as the needs of failing students. The format will vary from district to district, but as a classroom teacher, you will be asked to describe the materials you use, alternative strategies you've tried with struggling students, professional development sessions you've attended, so on and so forth. It is a comprehensive plan and should take you a few hours to fill out. As with any paperwork, the better organized you are ahead of time, the easier this task will be!

■ **Special education forms relating to the Individualized Education Plan (IEP):** Before special education meetings, you will be asked to record student attendance and grades, provide a short narrative on performance, and assess the student's strengths and weaknesses. This will also take a few hours to fill out.

Planning, Paperwork, and Prioritizing

■ **Budget requests:** Believe it or not, these will be due in October for the following school year! The forms can be a bit tedious, as can wading through all of the catalogs. In September and October, spend one lunch or prep period per week at your desk, flipping through and earmarking. It will be well worth it!

■ **Reading and math benchmarks:** These are the tests of progress for elementary school students, and they begin sometime toward the end of the first quarter. The form these tests take, and the process for administering them, will vary depending on your district. Before reaching the end of the first quarter, be sure to ask your principal how the benchmarks work in your school and if you will be receiving training.

■ **Permanent record cards:** At the end of the school year, you will be asked to once again record student attendance and performance for the year. A one-page form will be required for each student; the time it will take you to complete this task will depend 1) on the number of students you have and 2) whether or not you have your student folders in order.

Paperwork with a Purpose

We had to inventory all of our supplies. Too many teachers were "borrowing" things.

ASSISTANT PRINCIPAL, SAN FRANCISCO, CA

Always make copies of important documents, like observation evaluations. And don't be afraid to save or print out emails. This might not be the business world, but there's still the need to cover your behind!

SCIENCE TEACHER, NEW ROCHELLE, NY

When it comes time to complete permanent record cards, staying on top of the task all year will help tremendously. Also, sit with some fellow teachers while filling them out. The tedious can be made fun with a little touch of companionship!

68

WORLD HISTORY TEACHER, LOS ANGELES, CA

Getting Organized

Are you wondering how you're going to keep track of all these papers yet? If not, you should be! Your classroom is capable of running like a well-oiled machine. Without organization, though, that Lamborghini is sure to be a lemon. On the following pages you'll find what the Voices of Experience had to say on the topic.

teacher tip

Rolling file cabinets are a great idea! They are light enough and convenient enough to move from the computer in the staff lounge to a more comfortable work area in your own room, to be conveniently slid under a table during testing, or more permanently stored in a closet. Whether you're organizing student files or curriculum materials, rolling file cabinets are an organizational dream.

Be Well Equipped

I keep a three-ring binder for each class. In that binder I keep my lesson plans, any handouts used for that lesson, and notes on what worked and what didn't.

COMPUTER PROGRAMMING TEACHER, HEBRON, IN

Organization is a necessity for keeping your sanity as a teacher. Cubbies, baskets, bins, crates, baggies, bowls, cups, tins, boxes, file folders—you name it, I use it!

GIFTED AND TALENTED TEACHER, ANNISTON, AL

I use several pocket folders folded inside out and bound together on the nonfolded side. Then I label each pocket for a subject area. I have a weekly lesson plan page for each subject. I tuck any papers or materials that I will need for each subject behind the lesson plan page.

KINDERGARTEN TEACHER, MACON, GA

Your Schedule, Your Life

BlackBerry, PalmPilot, doesn't matter. Just get some sort of Personal Digital Assistant to help you keep track of important dates and contact information. You can even link it to your computer!

MIDDLE SCHOOL PRINCIPAL, WATERBURY, CT

I use everything I can to keep my schedule straight: my desk blotter calendar, my computer, stickies, and highlighters.

FIRST-GRADE TEACHER, ST. PAUL, MN

My district has its calendar online. I printed one out at school and have it on the wall.

FIFTH-GRADE TEACHER, NEW HAVEN, CT

Prioritizing

One way veteran teachers are able to stay organized is by prioritizing. What you would like to accomplish and what you need to accomplish are two different things. Take care of needs before wants, and be careful not to neglect other aspects of your life. Remember that your students will need you as much in June as they do now. On the next few pages, experienced teachers will tell you how to accomplish this.

★ THE FACT OF THE MATTER ★

Compared to educators in 32 other industrialized nations, in 2001 American teachers spent 73 percent more time teaching their class which, by the end of the school year, equaled 59 extra eight-hour days of teaching.

Source: "Number of Teaching Hours per Year: 1996, 2001." Organization for Economic Cooperation and Development. 2001. http://www.oecd.org/dataoecd/1/25/14624887.xls.

Addressing What Needs to Be Done

I tried to get all of my grading done before I left school so that in the evening, I could concentrate on the next day's material.

ECONOMICS TEACHER, DEKALB, IL

My priority is always whatever directly impacts my students that day, such as copying homework so that it would be ready for that day or preparing materials for daily student activities.

FIRST-GRADE TEACHER, PITTSBURGH, PA

I did not prioritize. Instead I fought wildfires as I encountered them, which not only made the situation more stressful but also put a strain on my home life because I spent far too much (and all too often inefficient) time at school.

ENGLISH TEACHER, BISHOP, CA

73

" *Addressing What You Want to Get Done*

If you need it in the next hour, do it now; if you need it tomorrow, get it done before the end of the day; if you need it next week . . . save it for the weekend.

ENGLISH TEACHER, KIEL, WI

I come into school early to straighten papers and set out what I need for the day. I also sit and have a cup of coffee to ease into my day.

KINDERGARTEN TEACHER, ALBUQUERQUE, NM

Set up a good filing system with sections for each student, the curriculum, and memos and schedules of committee and staff meetings outside of work.

SCIENCE AND SOCIAL STUDIES TEACHER, METAIRIE, LA

Setting Limits

It is very important that you take your job seriously, but also that you do not fumble the ball at home. Your family, your friends, yourself—all of these are important if you are to be a happy, well-balanced teacher. It is possible: you *can* have a life at school and a life at home.

I set a limit on time after school: no more than three hours and then home. This is difficult because I'm always reluctant to leave until I feel I've given it my all, but I know how important it is to not overextend myself.

SECOND-GRADE TEACHER, BOSTON, MA

"

In retrospect, I think sticking to a schedule that included time to do things besides schoolwork, would have made me more effective as a teacher and less resentful of how little time I had for myself.

ENGLISH TEACHER, PORT ORCHARD, WA

I learned to allow myself one errand per day on my way home. Then, after dinner, I would work until 10:00 P.M., stopping not because I was done but because if I didn't allow an hour to wind down, I had trouble getting to sleep.

SOCIAL STUDIES TEACHER, BROOKLYN, NY

"

Please don't forget that the only good teacher is the teacher who is *still* teaching. By setting limits for yourself, you stand a much better chance of avoiding burnout and of joining the ranks of the Voices of Experience. Do it for yourself, but more importantly, do it for the students. In the next chapter, the veterans zero in on student issues and how to best deal with them so that everybody wins.

Planning, Paperwork, and Prioritizing

4

It's All for the Students

> I didn't realize I would be the scrutinized role model that I am. Kids even notice your shoes!
>
> *English teacher, Plymouth, MN*

Many teachers will pick up *Training Wheels for Teachers* and immediately turn to this chapter. The approach you take to teaching should be similar—always put the students first. Kids these days are carrying baggage far greater than their years and therefore require guidance in many areas, spanning everything from motivation to discipline.

The right teaching methods can help channel the energy of today's youth. Ensure that they are comfortable but challenged while in your classroom. They will most certainly learn from you; the trick is opening yourself up to learn from them. This chapter is here to help get the relationship started—time will do the rest!

Rules and Respect

It is important that newbies learn from veterans, but it's also important that they do not simply copy another teacher's system and style. It's your classroom: you have to believe in what you're teaching and how you're trying to teach it. That being said, there are some general guidelines to follow when making rules:

■ **Limit the number of rules.**

   Less is more when trying to establish the rules with your students.

■ **Make sure your rules comply with the school handbook.**

   Kids do not learn when they are given contradictory messages.

■ **Provide the rules in written form and then verbally reinforce them.**

   This will improve student comprehension.

■ **Include students when creating the classroom rules.**

If they have a say in the rules, they will have more respect for them.

■ **Send the rules home for a parent signature.**

This helps with reinforcement and in avoiding potential complaints down the road.

teacher tip

Often the most troublesome student is acting out just to get your attention. By paying the least amount of attention when the student is acting out and giving the student your undivided attention when she is behaving, you can reduce this negative behavior.

Emphasizing the Positive

We brainstorm the rules together the first day of school. I write them out and photocopy them for the students to bring home, the parents sign them, and they stay posted all year. Whenever a new student arrives, I have another student explain them. It's a good reminder for everyone.

PHYSICAL SCIENCE TEACHER, LA CROSSE, WI

When it comes to establishing classroom rules, I give my students choices, thus empowering them.

READING SPECIALIST, VANCOUVER, WA

Every day we review classroom rules along with a cheer. This method gets the students involved by using rhythm and chanting. During the day we cite examples and reward those students who are following the rules so that others will take notice.

FIRST-GRADE TEACHER, PHILADELPHIA, PA

Reinforce with Respect

I convince the students that they are *all* worthwhile and capable.

SCIENCE TEACHER, ORLANDO, FL

I address them politely, never lose my patience, never raise my voice, and tell them what I expect from them, not to mention what they can expect from me.

FOURTH-GRADE TEACHER, CHANDLER, AZ

I never talk down to my students but instead try to make them realize the consequences of their "poor choices."

LANGUAGE ARTS TEACHER, NEWARK, NJ

Be Firm and Consistent

Rules are meaningless as mere wall decorations. They have to be enforced consistently.

SIXTH-GRADE TEACHER, BRONX, NY

Explain, model, and justify with real examples of actions and their consequences. Kids need to know the practicality and purpose of rules.

FIFTH-GRADE TEACHER, BERLIN, CT

My first year, I was lucky enough to have a great assistant principal. He demanded that I follow through on whatever consequences I chose in disciplining the kids.

MATHEMATICS TEACHER, BALTIMORE, MD

85

Productive Discipline Versus Punitive Discipline

When it comes to discipline, there's a fine line that a teacher must walk: standing your ground while making sure you don't ruin a relationship. Here are a few effective methods for getting through to students who are acting out, and helping them find a way to not do "it" again!

■ Avoid embarrassing the student in any way, shape, or form, especially in front of peers.

■ Be firm, fair, and consistent; double standards and favoritism will cost you the respect of *all* of your students.

■ Remember that the student is upset, and when people are upset, they tend to lose their auditory skills!

■ Be very clear about why you are displeased.

■ Be very clear about what the specific action was and what the consequence will be.

■ Be very clear that you like the student, just not the behavior.

■ Deal with all issues in the classroom as a teacher; avoid slipping into friendship mode, even during the best of times.

Teacher ≠ Friend

So many new teachers come into the classroom wanting the students to like them and quickly find themselves being worked by the crowd because they are not tough enough.

MATHEMATICS, SCIENCE, AND READING TEACHER, ROANOKE, VA

I think I became too chummy with one of my students, to the point that he didn't respect me enough as an authority figure. It's okay to get familiar with students, but a professional distance must be maintained.

LANGUAGE ARTS TEACHER, SAN FRANCISCO, CA

Part of being the adult in the relationship is drawing emotional boundaries. The kids need you as a good adult role model more than they need you as a friend.

SPECIAL EDUCATION TEACHER, PORTLAND, OR

Effective Discipline

Feel comfortable and confident in enforcing your discipline plan and start right away; it's amazing how the tone you set the first week can affect your entire school year.

GLOBAL STUDIES TEACHER, CHICAGO, IL

When rules are broken, I separate the student from the environment. Give the student a time out in the corner, in the hall, or even in the principal's office.

FOURTH-GRADE TEACHER, BRONX, NY

I am firm regarding boundaries, but also nurturing. After the consequence, I revisit the issue, just to make sure the student understands what happened and why.

FIRST-GRADE TEACHER, MADISON, WI

Making Mistakes and Atoning for Them

One reason to be a firm but forgiving teacher is that sometimes it's *you* who makes the mistake! The possibilities are innumerable, but below you will find a list of examples. In considering both the specifics and "the big picture," keep in mind that the approach taken in one situation can often be applied to another. Be sure to follow through on promises just like you would with consequences, and good luck!

■ **You wrongly accuse a student of doing something she did not do.**

Don't hesitate to apologize and explain; she should know why you accused her and also what led you to jump to that conclusion. Don't be afraid to ask for her help in identifying the real offender.

■ **You make an inappropriate joke or use an inappropriate name with a student.**

You need to apologize to him, and if the joke was made in front of peers, the apology should also be made in front of these peers. If the joke or name was extremely inappropriate, you need to inform your principal and begin the damage control.

■ **You reprimand a student and then decide that you were harsher than necessary.**

Focus on mending the relationship; you don't necessarily need to apologize, but you should do a little bit of "makeup" work. If a parent or administrator criticizes you for overreacting, calmly explain how you felt at that moment and why. Also, explain how you plan on handling that kind of situation in the future.

Once you start on this path of confident modesty, you'll find it isn't too hard to maintain control while allowing students to see that you are indeed human. One unintended benefit is that you are showing the students how to deal with their own mistakes.

Avoiding Mistakes with Special Education Students

Schools welcome all sorts of students with the promise of an education and time with their peers. These include students who require special education support. Special ed has become one of the most time-consuming, energy-draining, budget-consuming aspects of teaching. Children with special needs require individualized treatment, and the following is a list of how to handle situations specific to these kids:

- **Don't develop your own special education accommodations.** Be sure to follow the Individualized Education Plan (IEP), because oftentimes teachers do too much to help these students, thus making them less self-sufficient.

- **Don't ever recommend medication to a parent.** It isn't your area of expertise, and in most cases, the things that a school employee suggests must be paid for by the district.

- **Watch your words very carefully.** Oftentimes, kids with processing problems miss subtleties and other social cues.

- **Don't wait to address a student's needs.** If you think a student may have an undiagnosed disability, let your principal know.

- **Review the IEP before giving out your quarterly grades.** There might be special considerations made for certain students.

91

Opportunities Missed

After a shouting match, rather than reflecting on her actions, the student focused on the fact that I had spoken inappropriately to her and so dismissed any responsibility for her actions.

SPECIAL EDUCATION TEACHER, SCOTTSDALE, AZ

An angry student stood to hit me. I immediately took his hand and turned it behind his back. I told the student that he'd better not "mess with me." I didn't model an appropriate response, because violence only begets violence.

MAGNET FUNDS COORDINATOR, NEW HAVEN, CT

I told a disruptive student to "shut up." He told me that wasn't a nice thing to say, and I apologized. Maintaining relationships is so important in teaching.

KINDERGARTEN TEACHER, ST. LOUIS, MO

When I first started as a teacher, I made the mistake of constantly asking the assistant principal for help rather than handling the student myself. I learned that it was better to deal with what I could in the classroom and save the front office for truly horrible situations.

ASSISTANT PRINCIPAL, LAFAYETTE, LA

I work hard and let them know it. When I make a mistake, I admit it. When I don't know the answer, I say so and assure them that I will find the answer.

MATHEMATICS TEACHER, WHITNEY POINT, NY

Atoning for Those Mistakes

I humiliated one student in front of his peers by using his work as an example of what <u>not</u> to do. It took an entire year to repair that relationship.

KINDERGARTEN TEACHER, SOUTH GATE, CA

I gave an F to a student who had no idea it was coming. I stood behind the grade but apologized for not making the parents aware of the problem sooner. Now grades are sent home weekly and must be signed. This puts the responsibility on parents and students to keep up with a drop in grades.

FOURTH-GRADE TEACHER, KENNESAW, GA

It's All for the Students

I judged a new student by his first-day behaviors. He was nervous and trying to win friends with defiance and disobedience. I put his chair close to mine and told him every time he was on task how proud I was. He began to want to please me rather than his classmates.

SECOND-GRADE TEACHER, WOODRIDGE, IL

I used to misinterpret quietness as comprehension. I learned to look for understanding from all students, not just the ones who seek assistance.

MATHEMATICS TEACHER, AURORA, IL

95

How to Hold Their Attention

Part magic, part Broadway, part perspiration, and part inspiration—these are the things that go into holding court over a room full of jesters, dreamers, introverts, extroverts, brainiacs, and maniacs! Here are some tricks of the trade that will help *you* hold court in a classroom of any age:

■ After a student contributes, call on another student to agree, disagree, or simply comment on what the first student said.

■ Have an item to pass around during discussions; the students know they can only speak if they have it. (Remember the conch shell in *Lord of the Flies*?)

■ "Dipstick" (ask "on the spot" comprehension questions) during discussion, making sure everyone is following along. The Socratic method—teaching by asking specific, guided questions—is one example.

■ Follow the Rule of Seven: change the activity or at least the point of attention every seven minutes.

■ Use a timer as a definitive signal to end an activity, so that kids have a way of checking how much time they have left.

- Have "stop talking and look at me" clap and response signals in place from day one.

- Hand signals (for the bathroom, water, etc.) minimize interruptions.

- Use various multisensory approaches to appeal to all of the learning styles of students in your classroom; differentiated instruction is the way to go in the age of heterogeneity. Howard Gardner's multiple intelligences is one example.

- Think back to when you were a child—what did your teachers do that got your attention? Chances are, the same tricks still work!

teacher tip

Howard Gardner's eight "intelligences" include Linguistic (word smart), Logical-Mathematical (number/reasoning smart), Spatial (picture smart), Bodily-Kinesthetic (body smart), Musical (music smart), Interpersonal (people smart), Intrapersonal (self smart), and Naturalist (nature smart). To read an NEA interview with Mr. Gardner, visit http://www.nea.org/neatoday/9903/gardner.html.

Utilizing Your Students

"Children are innately curious, like to feel accepted, and generally want to share their own experiences. Using their names and connecting the topic of discussion to personal experiences is helpful. Tapping into their natural curiosity and using age-appropriate humor are some hooks that help kids stay involved.

FIRST-GRADE TEACHER, MONTGOMERY VILLAGE, MD

Every week, a student serves as "president." This honor gives her several responsibilities, including acting as leader during discussions. Most students respect the president, since they know they will be in front of the class one day.

HISTORY TEACHER, OGDEN, UT

I pair up students, ask a question, and have the students discuss it with their partner and then share with the group.

SPECIAL EDUCATION TEACHER, DES MOINES, IA

Mass Appeal

The lesson has to be something that the students can relate to, have prior knowledge of, and an interest in. Give them the opportunity to feel successful.

SPANISH TEACHER, DEER PARK, TX

Know their world and tap into it.

MIDDLE SCHOOL ENGLISH TEACHER, SOUTH BEND, IN

Don't just teach facts. Teach how to think. I tell them we will learn the whats, wheres, whens, and whos only to use as tools to learn the whys and hows.

SOCIAL STUDIES TEACHER, BROOKLYN, NY

Nobody Said School Can't Be Fun!

Sometimes when we do calendar, I pretend that the kids are on *The Price is Right*. The kids love to applaud when another student does something right.

SPECIAL EDUCATION TEACHER, KNOXVILLE, TN

I use a "whiz bang" in the middle of the discussion; saying something loudly or in a crazy voice usually does the trick.

GOVERNMENT TEACHER, LAS VEGAS, NV

I use music, singing, rhyming, interactive clapping, and physical motions to quiet them down and hold their attention.

FIRST-GRADE TEACHER, PHILADELPHIA, PA

One tip is to stand on a box when you are saying something very important. It can be your "soapbox."
FIFTH- THROUGH EIGHTH-GRADE TEACHER, EAST AMHERST, NY

I let them believe that I hadn't thought of what they just added to the conversation. They love it!

ENGLISH TEACHER, PLYMOUTH, MN

Motivational Tools and Methods

Like the students themselves, motivation comes in all shapes and sizes. The ultimate motivator is the intrinsic reward, but in order to keep the kids under control, it behooves you to have some meaningful, extrinsic motivators in place from the get-go. Just as with discipline, you must be prepared to follow through on whatever has been promised. With consistency and proper planning, the motivators will become intrinsic without you even noticing it; and by definition, isn't that what these kinds of genuine, inherent rewards are all about?

Intrinsic Motivators

The *Webster's New World Dictionary* defines *intrinsic* as follows: "Belonging to the real nature of a thing; not dependent on external circumstances; essential; inherent."

Five Ways to Intrinsically Motivate Your Students

1. Establish a positive classroom climate.

2. Help students feel that they are part of the classroom community.

3. Give frequent, timely, positive feedback to encourage students.

4. Ensure opportunities for students' success by giving assignments that are neither too easy nor too difficult.

5. Help students find personal meaning and value in the material. "Making a connection" is always key!

Source: The Center for Support of Teaching and Learning at Syracuse University. 2004. http://cstl.syr.edu/.

Positive Reinforcement

I find that *specific* praise is the best motivation.

MATHEMATICS TEACHER, SAN FRANCISCO, CA

People are happier when they are gently motivated to raise the bar for themselves.

COMPUTER SCIENCE TEACHER, FOUNTAIN, CO

I let the students know that I empathize with them, and I reward them for doing a good job. I tell them how important they are to me and make a big deal about them being absent and tell them that I missed them.

SPECIAL EDUCATION TEACHER, INDIANAPOLIS, IN

Listening to student responses helps me to meet students at their individual achievement levels and to cue into their interests to motivate them.

SPECIAL EDUCATION TEACHER, HARRISBURG, PA

Extrinsic Motivators

The *Webster's New World Dictionary* defines *extrinsic* as follows: "Not really belonging to the thing with which it is connected; not inherent; being, coming, or acting from the outside; extraneous."

Five Ways to Extrinsically Motivate Your Students

1. Free Pass: This allows a student to skip a homework assignment or quiz.

2. Snack: Healthy is better, but tasty is best!

3. Treasure Box: Offer an age-appropriate treat when a student has consistently done the right thing.

4. Certificate of Achievement: Everybody likes to have something for Mom or Dad to hang on the fridge!

5. Responsibility: Ask a student to do a class job, run an errand, etc.; anything that shows the trust they have earned.

Teacher tip While you're at it, why not decide who gets the reward with a student vote? Let the class decide who's most deserving—99 times out of 100, you'll agree!

Tangible Rewards

The Desk Fairy visits from time to time, and if a student has a neat desk, she leaves them a sticker.

GIFTED AND TALENTED TEACHER, SYLVANIA, OH

I have a noodle jar in the classroom with a sign on it, "Use your noodle to earn one." The class can earn noodles that they add to a jar. Once the jar is full, the class gets a reward. They can see the jar filling up, and that provides them with incentive to earn more.

SPECIAL EDUCATION TEACHER, CHARLESTON, SC

I have a place in my room called "Paradise." Sand, beach chair, desk, lemonade, and a tropical painting behind a curtain of beads. Students work to buy an afternoon in Paradise!

HISTORY TEACHER, WOODLAND PARK, CO

The students work for chain links (they can see the chain getting longer and longer) that translate into rewards.

PRE-K THROUGH SECOND-GRADE TEACHER, FRANKLIN, MN

Cooperative learning is the best way to motivate your students. Students love working with their peers, and everyone is successful in group work.

HISTORY TEACHER, PORTLAND, OR

The biggest motivator I have is posting the "most improved" list on my classroom door; whether it's for a quiz, a test, or the quarter.

SOCIAL STUDIES TEACHER, TONAWANDA, NY

"I have a lot of individual incentives, table incentives, and a class incentive. If a kid blows the individual incentive for the day, there is always something else to stay on track for.

READING TEACHER, NORFOLK, VA

I developed an award system called "wizard cards." Students earn one every time they're well behaved. They may be redeemed for any number of things, such as a skipped assignment, extra points, a choice place to sit, or extra library time.

KINDERGARTEN TEACHER, TALLAHASSEE, FL

I expect students to speak Spanish whenever possible. When they slip and use English, they get "el gato." This is a cat puppet and is used like a hot potato; it is passed around the room whenever English is spoken. It really makes the students listen to one another.

SPANISH TEACHER, BALTIMORE, MD

It's All for the Students

This chapter spoke to some of the issues you'll face with students, but remember that interacting with parents is a part of your job as well. In less affluent districts, teachers complain about too little parental involvement; in wealthy districts, about too much. There is no happy medium, but all good teachers learn how to involve caregivers (Mom, Dad, Grandma, Aunt, etc.) in a positive manner. Channel their energy, just as you do the students'. The next chapter will show you how.

5

Teaming Up with Parents

> Don't put off returning the phone calls of a pushy parent. The longer you wait, the longer they have to think of new questions!
>
> *U.S. history and government teacher, Washington, DC*

When dealing with primary caregivers, there is one piece of advice you should remember: It *always* pays to establish a relationship with parents from day one. Frequent, positive communication with parents is the key to helping their child get the best education possible. This chapter will take you through the different kinds of parents you'll meet and how to work closely with them all—including how to handle that first parent-teacher conference (and the hordes of inquisitive caregivers you'll talk to there)!

Quality Communication

The number one way to get—and keep—parents involved is to open the lines of communication from the get-go. This will take some extra effort on your part but will be well worth it in the end. Research shows that students whose parents are involved in their child's education experience greater rates of success. The goal is to establish effective, *two-way* communication. Here are some methods for doing so:

■ **Make phone calls, even if you're just going to leave a message.** Share some good news and let the folks at home get to know the sound of your voice. Make sure you always have the most up-to-date phone number for each of your students.

■ **Send letters home with a sign-off if necessary.** This will help remind parents about upcoming events or the due dates for projects.

■ **Have students make homework folders** that constantly travel back and forth between home and school.

113

■ **Write newsletters, or better yet, have the students do it!** The focus can be anything from a summary of the past month to upcoming events; individual highlights or classwide achievements!

■ **Make the parent handbook available.** This should be provided by the school and should contain policies, procedures, important dates, and a code of conduct.

■ **Attend schoolwide events.** Whether they be athletic, academic, or social, these events give parents and teachers the chance to build relationships and earn trust. As much as it is important for parents to know about these gatherings, it is important for a new teacher to attend.

■ **Give weekly or monthly awards.** These can be noted with a certificate and given out for things like good citizenship or perfect attendance. They serve as a message to parents (and students) that the student is doing a good job!

■ **Make home visits.** If attendance is a problem, home visits can be very effective. Let parents know that you want their child—that you *need* their child—in school every day. Also, remind them that truancy officers are automatically alerted once a student has missed ten days.

■ **Offer Saturday seminars** aimed at helping parents help their kids.

■ **Utilize interpreters.** Sometimes you'll need to team up with a colleague who is fluent in another language to communicate with a parent. If no one is available to help, let your principal know that there is a communication gap.

★ THE FACT OF THE MATTER ★

Researchers report that parent participation:

1) enhances children's self-esteem, 2) improves children's academic achievement,

3) improves parent-child relationships, and 4) helps parents develop positive attitudes toward school and a better understanding of the schooling process.

Source: Patricia Clark Brown. "Involving Parents in the Education of Their Children." ERIC Clearinghouse on Teaching and Teacher Education, 1989.
http://www.ericfacility.net/ericdigests/ed308988.html

Miscommunication

Give parents every opportunity to teach you about their child.

SCIENCE TEACHER, MILWAUKEE, WI

Sometimes there is a breakdown in communication: the child is telling the parent one thing when something else is actually true. Communication is key with parents.

SOCIAL STUDIES AND ENGLISH TEACHER, WAPPINGERS FALLS, NY

If there's a chance the first notice was overlooked, be sure to send a second notice. If there's a chance the student erased your first message, call again. Getting over these obstacles takes a lot of work, but once contact is finally made, it's well worth the effort. **THIRD-GRADE TEACHER, TORONTO, CANADA**

The conspiracy of adults has all but disappeared. These days, people are all too willing to defend their kids and distrust other adults. That can't be the case with teachers and parents. Only by establishing this "conspiracy" can you stay one step ahead of the kids. **FOURTH-GRADE TEACHER, ANN ARBOR, MI**

116

More Ears, Less Mouth!

Always allow the parent to ask the first question. You get their "tone" that way, and it will frequently keep you from sticking your foot in your mouth.

MATHEMATICS TEACHER, BRONX, NY

I wish I wasn't so arrogant during my first year. I didn't know much and definitely didn't know how to talk to parents about their child. I should have spent some time asking questions rather than just talking.

ENGLISH TEACHER, MELBOURNE, FL

Never miss a chance to keep your mouth shut!

LANGUAGE ARTS TEACHER, ROCK POINT, AZ

117

Put It in Writing

At the start of each month, I give an outline of things to come (themes, projects, etc.) and most importantly, I have a sign-and-return portion on the bottom so that I know the parent saw it.

FIFTH-GRADE TEACHER, BERLIN, CT

I send home very detailed progress reports every week so that parents are always in the loop.

SOCIAL STUDIES AND READING TEACHER, OAKLAND, CA

A simple form letter, just slightly personalized to reflect individual performance, usually does the trick.

LANGUAGE ARTS TEACHER, HALES CORNERS, WI

Parents expect to be called for everything. Instead, I have learned how to make good use of agenda planners (all our students are required to purchase one). I write notes home in them; it helps to make students accountable, and it's a good way to keep track of your attempts to communicate.

SPANISH TEACHER, TRENTON, NJ

E.T. Phone Home!

Most of the difficulties that I've had with parents have been because I didn't call home soon enough after problems began.

SPANISH TEACHER, CONVERSE, IN

Although I frequently write notes home, you just can't beat a phone call. More times than not, I learn something about the student that I never would have imagined!

KINDERGARTEN TEACHER, ALBUQUERQUE, NM

I find that once you get a parent talking, you learn a lot of valuable information. The look in a kid's eyes is always priceless, too, once you reveal something you know.

FOURTH-GRADE TEACHER, ROCKVILLE, MD

I always struggle with having enough contact with parents. I find that I reach some parents better with email than with the phone.

LANGUAGE ARTS TEACHER, BEACHWOOD, OH

Involving the Parents

You will meet many different types of parents along the way, and each parent requires a different approach. Here are the general "parent prototypes" and what you can do to try and build a positive, productive relationship with them:

■ **Yippy the Promising Parent:** *will sell you the moon but deliver nada, zip, zilch! These folks may talk a good game, but they never do the things with their child that they say they will.*

Your best approach with Yippy is to make him accountable; sign-off sheets and specific instructions attached to papers and projects (example: "Please help your child to edit the rough draft that is to be submitted with the final essay") are recommended.

■ **Mr. and Mrs. Directed:** *whose efforts are well intentioned but oh so misdirected. For example, the mother who takes Christmas away from her child because he received one bad grade. On a practice quiz.*

Try to get this parent to use positive reinforcement by providing not only examples of constructive rewards, but also lots of opportunities to give those rewards (for example, sending home complimentary notes).

■ **All's Well That Means Well:** *has a big heart, but the student rarely gets any help; the parent can't make it to conference night because he has to work but will appear 10 minutes into your lesson the next day and want to discuss Junior's grades.*

Your best approach with Means Well is to be accommodating. Be thankful when a parent really wants to help!

■ **My Kid Matters Most:** *goes to no end to make sure that all the support (and then some) is there for her child, even if it's at the expense of the other students.*

Your best approach with My Kid is to show her your class *in action;* not only will she see how lucky *her* child is and how much he matters to you, My Kid will also come to understand, hopefully, that you aren't a one-on-one tutor.

■ **The Invisible Parent:** *You won't see this parent on the first day of school, at conferences, when his child has to go home with the chicken pox, or at any other point.*

Be as nice as possible to the student, as she really needs it! The parent who is invisible at school tends to be invisible at home. You can't do much about the home life, but give Invisible every opportunity to participate in his child's education: flyers for events, phone call invitations, anything to make him feel welcome!

■ **It's No Big Deal:** *Nothing ever really bothers her—nothing!*

If a problem is serious (example: a potential learning disability), do your best to convince NBD that her attention and participation are important; talk about the short-term solutions as well as the long term. It also helps to have other educators present to reinforce what you're saying—this way, she knows that this isn't just one teacher's opinion.

■ **Attorney for the Defense:** *Not guilty! No way, no how—not my child!*

For the parent of the child who can do no wrong, bring along all of the evidence you can gather: test scores, samples of work, grades from other teachers; whatever it takes to minimize this parent's wiggle room. It's important that you show Attorney that *every* child has strengths but also weaknesses that can be worked on.

Meet 'Em Half Way

"

At night, I hold free parent workshops to best help the parents deal with issues at home.

LANGUAGE ARTS TEACHER, MIAMI, FL

I had parents who looked at me as a baby-sitter because when the student was with me, she wasn't their concern. I dealt with these issues by getting the parents involved with their child's education at whatever level they were ready and able.

SPECIAL EDUCATION TEACHER, MERRILLVILLE, IN

My expectations for student achievement were too high according to some parents. I had to educate them just as I did the students.

KINDERGARTEN TEACHER, FAWN GROVE, PA

Most parents who have a problem want to vent a bit before you get down to the crux of the issue. So let them vent and then try to set them at ease. Look for a compromise, although sometimes you do have to stick to your guns.

TEACHER LEADERSHIP INSTRUCTOR, OXFORD, OH

"

Put Things in Perspective

Being thick-skinned and patient with demanding parents wins a lot more battles than trying to be confrontational.

SCIENCE TEACHER, RICHMOND, VA

My biggest problem has been parents who want their children to make all A's. They're not really concerned about how their child learns; just with seeing that grade on the report card. Remind them that mistakes are learning opportunities and it never hurts to have something to work toward.

SPECIAL EDUCATION TEACHER, JOHNSON CITY, TN

I try to explain that grades don't reflect the entire child.

GIFTED CLASSES TEACHER, SYLVANIA, OH

Some parents have unrealistic opinions of their child's progress and place the blame for failure on me. Have clear reasons for each grade you give. Amazingly enough, though, it is often the student who sets his parents straight with the truth!

MATHEMATICS TEACHER, STATEN ISLAND, NY

It seemed, sadly enough, that many parents were ready to believe their child was not performing well in school. Most found it hard to believe that their child was successful at anything. Celebrate the successes and make sure Mom and Dad know how wonderful their child is with phone calls home.

COMPUTER TECHNOLOGY TEACHER, KERNVILLE, CA

Many parents are so frustrated with their inability to manage their own children that I end up being a parent coach as well as a teacher. When I started, I was 22 and single. I had no idea how to be a parent. I just used common sense.

FOURTH-GRADE TEACHER, ST. LOUIS, MO

Avoiding Confrontation

Some parents are near-impossible to get through to. But don't give up. Know that if you're successful with even a mere 25 percent of these caustic caregivers, it means you'll have helped that many more students. Just don't forget to take the "high road" to happiness:

■ **Remain professional.** Make sure to have at least two positive things to say about the student.

■ **Remain professional.** Don't take heated words personally.

■ **Remain professional.** Provide the necessary documentation and document what is said during the meeting.

■ **Remain professional.** Choose your words carefully as you construct a solution rather than deconstruct the particulars of the parent's complaint[s].

■ **Remain professional.** Inform your principal about a confrontation in a calm, concise manner. If necessary, ask that he or she join you at the next meeting with the parent.

Did I mention that you should remain professional?

Document, Document, Document!

Just because a parent is quiet doesn't mean that he is pleased. If a student is having problems, be sure to document what those problems are and what is being done to address them.

RELIGION TEACHER, MIDDLEBURG, VA

Write down everything that happens in meetings with parents and have parents sign the notes. Keep complete records.

FOURTH-GRADE TEACHER, BROOKSVILLE, FL

One parent disagreed with an action I took involving her child and wrote me a nasty letter. I made a copy of the letter and gave it to my principal so she would know what was going on. I now keep all copies of correspondence with parents and notes on our phone conversations.

SIXTH-GRADE TEACHER, ANAHEIM, CA

Grace Under Pressure

I've always found it difficult to remain calm when being verbally attacked by a parent. I learned to deal with it by putting the conversation on hold.

GEOGRAPHY TEACHER, ROCKPORT, MA

I have learned that if a parent becomes confrontational to notify an administrator, and to simply stop discussing the issue. You *do not* have to be harassed by an angry parent.

AMERICAN HISTORY TEACHER, PHILADELPHIA, PA

One parent was mentally ill and could not handle anything I told her. If a teacher knows about cases such as these, he is better off having additional people in the room during conferences. This is protective for the teacher, but it is also productive in that it can be an effective way to communicate so that all parties involved are better served.

SCIENCE TEACHER, OGDEN, UT

Walk a Mile . . .

Many parents have had bad experiences in school, and it takes time to gain trust. With trust comes understanding.

SOCIAL STUDIES TEACHER, CHARLESTON, SC

Lack of interest is often really lack of knowledge; parents aren't born knowing how to help their own children, especially if their parents didn't help them.

SPECIAL EDUCATION TEACHER, ORLANDO, FL

I always remind myself that when it comes to whether or not I should stick to my guns, there is a difference between following standards and being stubborn.

FIFTH-GRADE TEACHER, DAYTON, OH

129

TRAINING WHEELS FOR TEACHERS

The First Parent-Teacher Conference

When it's time for your first parent-teacher conference, you may be stressed and you may be nervous, but remember that the parents are, too, so do your best to set them at ease. In the process, you're liable to set yourself at ease as well! Here are some tips:

- **Be friendly but in command.** Don't let parents steer you away from your concerns, but smile while keeping the conversation on track.

- **Remember to sandwich.** A negative comment about a student will always seem less harsh between two positive comments.

- **Have all relevant documents on hand.** Whether it be grades, samples of work and tests, or attendance, have specific remedies in mind if there seems to be a concern.

■ **Document what is said if there seems to be a problem.** The first thing every principal asks when you report a problem with a student or parent is if you have a record of conversations. Paper trail, paper trail, paper trail. Make one!

■ **Be fair to everyone, yourself included, and stick to a time limit.** Indicate what the limit is in your flyer or newsletter and then have a timer on your desk. In stressful situations, it always helps if you can make things humorous, so something like a frog-shaped alarm clock that croaks will work wonders!

teacher tip A Voice of Experience from Arizona suggests having "student-led conferences." This helps make the students accountable for themselves, and by stepping back and acting as the facilitator, you will be better able to help parents understand their child's strengths and weaknesses.

Keeping Everyone Up-to-Date

Prior to the first conference, I send home a parent survey. I ask them to tell me what they need to know about, what they want to discuss, what they expect to hear, and what they can share. This allows me to individualize each conference.

THIRD-GRADE TEACHER, CHASKA, MN

Be ready to justify your grading system and start the conversation by thanking the parents for taking the time to talk with you.

MATHEMATICS TEACHER, SAN FRANCISCO, CA

I wish I had communicated more that I cared about their child and that I knew their child could learn. When I first started teaching, I was too focused on data.

SPECIAL EDUCATION TEACHER, SPRINGFIELD, VA

132

In some cases, I've asked for other teachers who teach the student to sit in on conferences with the parent to support my evidence. READING AND MATHEMATICS TEACHER, CINCINNATI, OH

We are most successful when we keep the focus on what the child is doing, what we need the child to do, and how the parent can support this.

ASSISTANT PRINCIPAL, DANVILLE, PA

Parents tend to believe what their children say. I try to help them see things from my perspective. I start by saying that I always do what I feel is in the child's best interest; if not in the near-term, then for the future. MATHEMATICS TEACHER, ROYSE CITY, TX

Parents need to feel as though their child is being made a top priority.

SECOND-GRADE TEACHER, NORFOLK, VA

I am a very blunt person, and I have to remember that I should sometimes temper what I say and to put a positive spin on it if possible. CREATIVE WRITING TEACHER, SALEM, SC

Be Confident!

At my first parent conference, I felt like I was a student again and that the parent was lecturing me. I didn't stand up for myself, or what I felt was best for the student.

THIRD-GRADE TEACHER, LAKE PARK, FL

I wish I had been more trusting of my judgments and instincts. I was too ready to assume I'd done things incorrectly. **ENGLISH TEACHER, PORT ORCHARD, WA**

I was taught long ago that body language is important to the successful outcome of a conference. I try to minimize stress by copying movements: if a parent leans toward me, I do the same; if they move back, I do, too. It's amazing how well this works to calm otherwise stressful situations.

ENGLISH AND SOCIAL STUDIES TEACHER, SAN DIEGO, CA

134

Parents try to blame the teacher for grades, but as one wise teacher told me, "Teachers don't fail students, students fail themselves."

HEALTH TEACHER, MOTLEY, MN

Accentuate the Positive

I tell parents that I want the best for their kids, just like they do. I am another stakeholder in their child's success.

LANGUAGE ARTS TEACHER, CHANNAHON, IL

Parents can be extremely defensive of their children, although the very same child drives them crazy at home! I try to praise the child in several ways before attempting to share an area of needed growth.

SPECIAL EDUCATION TEACHER, PHILADELPHIA, PA

Good Things Can Happen!

Collaboration is key: some of my most successful teaching relationships have been with parents.

FIFTH-GRADE TEACHER, SARASOTA, FL

A rocky road can get smoother and smoother if you just grease the skids a bit. Compliments go a long way, as does tactful honesty.

GOVERNMENT TEACHER, CHAPPAQUA, NY

I have lost a couple of kids whose parents never came through, but I have been successful with so many others. It has been my experience that parents come through more often than not.

FIRST-GRADE TEACHER, CORAL GABLES, FL

Almost as nice as hearing a "Thank you" from a student is hearing it from a parent, especially one who gave me a hard time early on. There are so many ways to feel vindicated as a teacher.

ASSISTANT PRINCIPAL, HARTFORD, CT

Teaming Up with Parents

In any people-driven industry, communication is of the utmost importance. And, as you read in this chapter, part of the job is establishing positive relationships with parents. The same can be said of colleagues. The next chapter provides helpful hints on getting along with your coworkers.

137

6

Communicating with Your Colleagues

> We helped each other with our weaknesses and shared our strengths.
>
> *Gifted classes teacher, Sylvania, OH*

Although you are in the classroom by yourself, successful teaching really comes as part of a team effort. That team includes your fellow teachers, the administration, and the dozens of other people who work in your building!

There will be plenty of times when the majority of the staff bands together for a good cause, but in any situation where resources like time and money are limited, there are bound to be conflicts. Read on to learn how you can not only establish strong relationships with the people in your building but maintain these relationships through tough times. That way, the good times will be that much sweeter!

Building Positive Relationships with Coworkers

There is no doubt that you will be getting lots of help during your first 100 days, but who's to say you can't do some helping yourself? Not only can you provide support to your fellow newbies, but you can lend a hand to the veterans as well. As the Voices of Experience say, there's something to be learned from everyone. Just imagine a veteran who has to use a computer for the first time; I have no doubt he'll need a new teacher's help shortly after hitting the power button! Here are some tips to start you on your way to building bridges:

■ **Chip in!** Cover someone's duty (bus, hall, etc.) when she has an emergency. Don't hide from committee work.

■ **Take the time to talk.** You can't build relationships if you don't get to know people. Taking those five minutes to ask how someone's day is going will reward you tenfold in the future.

■ **Prove yourself to be a reliable, competent teacher.** The more teachers respect you, the better your relationships will be. And remember, don't make a promise you might not be able to keep.

■ **Show your fun side.** There is always a reserve of energy for fun events; call on that reserve, especially the first time you are invited to do something with your colleagues.

teacher tip No matter how tired they are, no matter how worn out, no matter how tough this particular school year is, more times than not, teachers will still speak lovingly of the students when out socially—so don't be surprised when you do it, too!

A Team Effort

I was fortunate enough to join a wonderfully tight, supportive staff. I felt good about how they welcomed me and also about how I was able to contribute after getting my bearings.

FOURTH-GRADE TEACHER, PHOENIX, AZ

I was blown away by the camaraderie. I think that the students could tell how much we all cared about each other, just as we cared about them.

SCIENCE TEACHER, YONKERS, NY

"

The veterans were amazingly helpful, and I made fast friends with some of the other new teachers. By June, we all felt like veterans, and when two new teachers came aboard the following September, we were there to help them.

ENGLISH TEACHER, RENO, NV

The efforts I made were more than rewarded. By showing myself to be a team player, I definitely made a good impression.

FIRST-GRADE TEACHER, NEW HAVEN, CT

Cliques and Envy

Some of my colleagues were not as enthusiastic as I was, so they made sarcastic remarks about what an eager beaver I was. I dealt with it by simply explaining how much I enjoyed teaching. If that was a problem, it wasn't <u>my</u> problem.

LANGUAGE ARTS TEACHER, ALBUQUERQUE, NM

Avoiding a scene is always key.   **SECOND-GRADE TEACHER, CENTRAL ISLIP, NY**

Figure out who is willing to share and who isn't. You'll find that the sharers are the best teachers and most worthy of your company, anyway.   **FIRST-GRADE TEACHER, KANSAS CITY, MO**

I have seen male science teachers express prejudice toward female science teachers. I have dealt with this by making every effort to express my opinions. If you allow these types of people to silence you, you will never gain any respect.

CHEMISTRY TEACHER, WESTERN SPRINGS, IL

145

66

In the Staff Lounge

Teacher gossip is very hurtful. Just let it go. That person will find another victim soon. In my case, I simply did the best I could to show that the rumors weren't true, remembering that my <u>actions</u> would speak louder than her <u>words.</u>

PHYSICS TEACHER, LAREDO, TX

The teachers thought I was reclusive and antisocial. In reality I was overwhelmed and exhausted. When I realized what they thought of me, I made an extra effort to talk in the teachers' lounge and attend happy hour events. This cleared the air pretty quickly, much to my relief—and they helped me organize myself so I wasn't so overwhelmed anymore!

FOURTH-GRADE TEACHER, ATLANTA, GA

99

Calling All Newbies

Chances are, your building won't be so big that you're never once lumped in the same room with the rest of the rookies—there *has* to be some sort of staff development at the beginning of the year. Use this time or lose this time!

Introduce yourself and let momentum carry you and your fellow newbies forward. Instant friendships are formed through shared experience, and all of you should certainly share! You'll find that fellow rookie teachers are an invaluable resource.

■ Keep in mind that you always have something in common with a fellow newbie, even if one of you is a 40-year-old science teacher and the other is a 22-year-old English teacher. As Dr. Martin Luther King Jr. once said, "We may have all come on different ships, but we're in the same boat now."

■ Be sure to talk about issues such as difficulties with students, how each of you plans lessons, and confusion over assessment.

■ When you make a discovery, the other new teachers will want to know. So don't forget to share!

■ From sharing potential graduate school programs, to grapevine gossip, to what that first observation (and subsequent principal evaluation) was like, you and your fellow newbies are a great support structure for one another.

teacher tip Teachers have at least one prep period every day. If a fellow newbie needs some coverage during your prep time, help out if you can. He will be eternally grateful!

Newbie Bonding

It was great to be able to compare ideas and share the frustrations of being a new teacher with other new teachers. It made me feel that I wasn't alone.

FOURTH-GRADE TEACHER, WASHINGTON, DC

We are all sponges just soaking up the school's atmosphere, and when we get together, we squeeze it all out so that everyone is as informed as possible.

WORLD STUDIES TEACHER, PORTLAND, OR

It felt great to be able to ask "dumb" questions of each other.

SECOND-GRADE TEACHER, LIVE OAK, FL

We carpooled to the university for our graduate classes.

FOURTH-GRADE TEACHER, FRESNO, CA

Sharing Ideas and More

We laughed, cried, vented frustrations, and hung out together. Just knowing that I wasn't the only one feeling overwhelmed helped me to face each day with a positive attitude.

THIRD-GRADE TEACHER, PEARL CITY, IL

There was a whole group of us, and we met almost weekly to compare notes and to share common problems, celebrate successes, and fix any failures. We became a tight-knit group and were able to use the combined knowledge to establish ourselves as successful first-year teachers.

LEADERSHIP TEACHER, OXFORD, OH

We were able to share all of the "grand" ideas that we knew would work. When they didn't, we were able to laugh at ourselves.

LANGUAGE ARTS TEACHER, CONYERS, GA

Tapping Into the Veterans

Words cannot express the gratitude you will feel toward those helpful veterans for all the support they'll lend. You'll be willing to iron their clothes, wash their cars, do their taxes; that's how much you'll appreciate their help (before, after, and even during school!). On the next few pages, the Voices of Experience weigh in on the different ways that the veteran teachers have become an invaluable resource to them.

Knowledge from Those Who Know

A veteran teacher taught me all about the labor contract. No new teacher has time for these kinds of things, and all of a sudden I understood what I was responsible for and at what point things "crossed the line."

LANGUAGE ARTS TEACHER, MIAMI, FL

Veteran teachers are the best resource in the world, and they are usually thrilled to pass on their wealth of knowledge. They know all the shortcuts to help you keep your sanity. They know whom to ask for supplies, paperwork, information, etc. And they truly understand what it is like to be in your shoes!

EIGHTH-GRADE TEACHER, MANSFIELD, OH

Veterans helped me stay sane by reminding me that I wasn't going to be the immediate hero that I thought I would be; that I wouldn't be able to reach every child; and that no matter how hard I worked, there would be some students whom I wouldn't be able to motivate.

CHARACTER EDUCATION TEACHER, CHICAGO, IL

I worked with one teacher who saved my life. He talked me through lesson plans, walked me through how to handle parent conferences, and kept me from quitting when I was discouraged.

FOURTH-GRADE TEACHER, CHANDLER, AZ

Veteran teachers taught me that the students will test you and that the way that you react is what makes the best impression.

AMERICAN HISTORY TEACHER, PHILADELPHIA, PA

The older teachers reminded me that it was important to survive and not feel guilty for not being the perfect teacher, because no one is her first year.

SPECIAL EDUCATION TEACHER, OAKLAND, CA

The veteran teachers helped me tremendously with keeping dates straight as far as meetings, deadlines, testing, and so on. They also helped with ideas for goals and professional development plans.

LANGUAGE ARTS TEACHER, INDIANAPOLIS, IN

My problem with the veterans was . . . THEY RETIRED!!! So many of those teachers were wonderful to work with.

SECOND-GRADE TEACHER, FLUSHING, NY

Ideas for the Classroom

I received a lot of support from veteran teachers. I observed them while they were teaching, and they observed me. They also modeled lessons in my classroom.

SOCIAL STUDIES TEACHER, OKLAHOMA CITY, OK

I received help in the form of suggestions for successful classroom management, copies of proven lesson plans, class materials, and moral support.

U.S. HISTORY AND ECONOMICS TEACHER, GENESEO, NY

One teacher down the hall was a great sounding board. Rather than telling me what to do, she asked the questions that made me come up with the answers.

LITERATURE TEACHER, MADISON, GA

The Other Adults in the Building

Schools are living, breathing, dynamic institutions of learning and growing. Not only will members of the support staff be helpful with your teaching, they are often very helpful with the students. Nothing says you can't invite a secretary or custodian in to help judge projects or even just listen to presentations. Tap into *all* of your school's resources!

- **The secretaries in the front office:** They are your greatest source of information and your greatest allies when times get tough with students, parents, or other teachers. They know everybody and everything that goes on in the building.
- **The principal's secretary:** The principal may be hard to track down, but this person will help get your questions answered.
- **The custodian:** The best classroom is a clean, well-stocked classroom! You will find yourself needing all sorts of materials, and the custodian will be able to help with everything from unlocking doors to carrying equipment.
- **The PTA (PTO, HSA, or PCC in some districts) president:** This person is a good liaison between school and family.
- **The nurse:** The kids get headaches—and so do you.

Getting to Know You

Don't make the first words you speak to the custodian or secretary be a request for a favor. Usually, the things you really need done aren't in their job description. But if you're pleasant and friendly to them, they'll usually do it anyway.

SOCIAL STUDIES TEACHER, JUNEAU, AK

Custodians are key to your success—they have the keys to every room closet in the building, and they hear what the kids are saying!

KINDERGARTEN TEACHER, SANTA MONICA, CA

Learning about the whole special education classification process was amazing, and I have the entire special education staff to thank, from the teachers, to the staff psychologist, to the social workers.

FIFTH-GRADE TEACHER, STROUDSBURG, PA

157

I spent a lot of time talking with the other staff members, like the nurse and the security guards. I've even had them participate in classroom activities. The kids like and respect them, and this has helped with everything from discipline to building community within our school.

U.S. HISTORY TEACHER, BINGHAMTON, NY

I have seen other teachers behave disrespectfully toward assistants and secretaries. I was embarrassed for them, but not sad when the old saying 'what comes around goes around' was proven once again! Schools really function on a favors-based system.

FIFTH-GRADE TEACHER, PEEKSKILL, NY

Impressing Your Principal

When asked his impression of principals and other supervisors, one of the Voices of Experience wrote, "As a first year teacher I didn't realize how much work they have to do and that I had to be pretty independent." It's true. The stresses that come along with being a building leader are immense, and when things go wrong, it's all on their heads. Keep this in mind before passing judgment on an action that a principal may take.

The best thing for you to do is show your support for the principal and how she is trying to lead her team. Here are a few things you can do to adjust to the style of your building leader:

■ **Conduct yourself in an appropriate manner.** Show up on time for school and for staff meetings. Dress the part and represent the school well—how you speak and act in school as well as away from the building is a reflection on the principal. Also, avoid gossip; you never know when something you say will come back to haunt you!

■ **Communicate clearly.** When presenting a problem, don't become emotional. You don't want the problem-solving session to become a problem unto itself! Never assume that the principal is already aware of the issues. Calmly explain.

159

■ **Show initiative.** When sharing a concern or disagreeing with a principal, always provide another course of action. It's negative to disagree, but it's constructive when you can offer a potential solution.

■ **Be friendly.** Now we're not saying attach your lips to the principal's rear end! However, it never hurts to ask how someone is doing. There's no reason to be intimidated—you're all working together toward a common goal. Good relations with the administration benefit not just you but your students.

■ **Invite your principal in for student presentations.** Administrators often get caught up in paperwork and the business of running the building. They'll appreciate the opportunity to spend some time with the kids and to get to know one of their teachers!

Your Observation

It just might be that the first time you really interact with your supervisor is during the observation process. The following list will guide you through the steps, providing a few helpful hints to make things go as smoothly as possible.

STEP ONE: You will be contacted regarding a pre-observation conference. At this meeting, your supervisor will discuss when the observation will take place and ask you for details regarding what you will teach that day and how.
    What you should do: Be prepared to talk about your unit and its objective, as well as the goals of this particular lesson. Include aspects of assessment and closure.

STEP TWO: Your supervisor will come and observe; sometimes the supervisor will stay for 15 minutes, sometimes for an hour. This is indicative of his schedule, not of your teaching!
    What you should do: First, don't let the stress of being under the microscope impact your classroom management style, especially discipline. The supervisor does not expect to see perfect kids! Second, keep an eye on the clock and do not forget the assessment (even if it's just pausing to ask a few comprehension questions) and the closure. And third, reach out to the unengaged student; supervisors love this!

STEP THREE: You will be contacted regarding a post-observation conference. At this meeting, you will review the write-up, discuss the positives and the negatives, and agree to sign the final draft. Even if your lesson was perfect, supervisors will always include at least one area for improvement.

What you should do: Sign away! However, if you are uncomfortable with a comment, don't sign anything. Your supervisor's observations may be set in stone, but you can attach a rebuttal. See your mentor or building steward (union representative) for advice.

STEP FOUR: You and your supervisor will sign the final draft of the observation write-up, and you will receive a copy.

What you should do: Keep a copy for yourself, but before putting it into your personnel file at home, *show everybody at home.* Congratulations! Someone has noticed what a fantastic job you are doing with the kids!

teacher tip During your first year, you will be officially observed at least three times. This does not mean that at other times administrators won't just pop in to watch. Always be prepared!

Making an Impression on Your Principal

Principals love a heads-up on both good and bad news. It only makes you look good if you keep the principal informed. Don't hide in your room!

FOURTH-GRADE TEACHER, ATLANTA, GA

Although this might seem obvious, I always made sure I was on time for school and especially for meetings. I let the principal get to know me.

SCIENCE TEACHER, RENO, NV

Being forthright does not mean you are a brown-noser. In my first year, I delicately shared an opinion with my principal, and in the end, I think it helped me get approved for a minigrant. He must have gotten the impression I was trustworthy!

SPANISH TEACHER, MT. VERNON, NY

163

Collaborating to Solve Problems

I was very nervous around my principal, and that translated into not doing well whenever he came into the room. Now I invite him to share in the classroom, which he appreciates.

LANGUAGE ARTS TEACHER, BEACHWOOD, OH

I was labeled the "troublemaker" because I was unofficially the spokesperson for the staff and would bring up matters of concern to the administration. I had to clarify that my intention was to improve our school and meet our students' educational needs.

ALGEBRA TEACHER, LOS ANGELES, CA

When I would be questioned about something I had done, I would often feel "called on the carpet." Now that I assume they are just seeking information, I can answer without getting defensive.

LANGUAGE ARTS AND SOCIAL STUDIES TEACHER, PRICE, UT

Once during an evaluation with my principal I said, "No one has ever offered to help me out." She was surprised. She said that I looked like I was doing fine and didn't need any help. In fact, I looked as though I'd resent any offers. I had no idea I presented that sort of image. I opened up after that conference and things got a lot better.

GEOMETRY TEACHER, SPOKANE, WA

Administrators like to be in the loop, so I send them a copy of my weekly newsletter for parents.

ENGLISH TEACHER, SPRINGDALE, AR

A "Leader" Versus an "Administrator"

I didn't think that the principal would be so nice and helpful. He was a real educational leader, and if not for him, I never would have made it through those first 100 days!

THIRD-GRADE TEACHER, LAKE PARK, FL

I have had wonderful educational leaders, but there was one assistant principal who was impossible to work with. Her "philosophy" included constantly demeaning students and teachers. We all did the best we could to stay out of her way and to make sure that the students still had a productive, pleasant educational experience.

MATH AND LANGUAGE ARTS TEACHER, BROOKLYN, NY

Some of the experienced teachers gave my ideas the cold shoulder. Once my principal realized that I was sincere and had an earnest focus on learning, she would present my ideas to the staff without telling them where the ideas came from. Later she would reveal the source!

THIRD-GRADE TEACHER, LAKE WALES, FL

When there is a leader in the building, you can really tell because he is still a <u>teacher</u> at heart. Cherish these people and work closely with them; there is a lot to learn. If an <u>administrator</u> is running the show, do your best to implement the wonderful things a leader would, like awards ceremonies for the kids and communication with the parents. Do all you can to make up for the absence of that <u>leader.</u>

FIRST-GRADE TEACHER, DES MOINES, IA

When Good Principals Go Bad

While most principals are willing to help you at every turn, there are always a few who can be difficult. Here are some examples of potential problems that might arise and how you can best handle them:

■ **You get no support during a recurrent discipline problem.** Develop a system of rewards and consequences specific to that student's needs. Meanwhile, try to get the parents on board. If this is a situation where there has been violence—or you fear there might be—give your building steward the details of what has taken place, and be sure to have written documentation (discipline referrals, etc.). You may be liable if someone gets hurt, so make sure that you have covered yourself legally.

■ **You do not have the resources to provide for your students, according to curriculum guides and the district and state assessments.** A letter to the principal means a paper trail of responsibility, which may jump-start action. Remember, the squeaky wheel usually gets the grease. Be squeaky!

■ **A principal sides with a parent over you (requesting, for example, that a grade be raised).** First, try to present a unified front. Your principal may have thought of something you hadn't considered. However, if you can't reach a compromise and you feel strongly about the grade, make sure you can justify your system of grading so that the disagreement isn't a poor reflection on you. These situations can be very frustrating, so keep in mind the old adage of losing the battle so that you can win the war!

■ **You are asked to do something that contradicts your position of "students as *the* priority" (repeating a professional development seminar, serving on a committee that meets during the school day, etc.).** Save your "Get Out of Jail Free" card and use it to do right by the students only in the most extenuating of circumstances. Most principals will gladly give you a break as long as you aren't constantly asking for these types of favors. (Don't be the little teacher who cries wolf!) In those cases where there is no compromise, simply do the best you can. This too shall pass.

When Everybody Pitches In

Principals are extremely busy and love the opportunity to block off part of their schedule for the kids. Give them enough time to plan, and most of them will do all they can to attend. Some of my best lessons have been conducted in the presence of, and with the help of, my principal.

LANGUAGE ARTS TEACHER, ATLANTA, GA

Few teachers understand the rigors of being a school administrator. Few administrators appreciate the difficulty of teaching by modern standards. A respectful appreciation for both sides is needed to resolve those issues that pit teachers and administrators against one another.

SPANISH TEACHER, PENSACOLA, FL

By talking to the principal ahead of time—whether about a problem or a fun event—I have been able to get her involved. It has made for a good working relationship with her and I think a better relationship between students and administration.

SPECIAL EDUCATION TEACHER, CINCINNATI, OH

The only thing more satisfying than a situation where I have done right by a student is a situation where a whole group of us has done right. There's nothing like a team effort, especially when the principal is on board!

MATHEMATICS TEACHER, PHOENIX, AZ

171

On a day-to-day basis, it's amazing how much goes on within a school. The brush fires that will pop up include everything from your first critical evaluation to concern over prejudice. Prejudice certainly qualifies as more than a brush fire, though. The next chapter will offer advice on how to utilize everyone's help, from colleagues to parents to the students themselves, to snuff these blazes out.

Ambrose Bierce once wrote that prejudice is a vagrant opinion without visible means of support. All too often, students experiment with their "vagrant opinions," and it's up to us to make sure they learn the appropriate lesson.

Second-grade teacher, West Haven, CT

A baby has yet to be born who dislikes someone because of his skin color, religion, nationality, or gender. Unfortunately, we live in a world that sometimes teaches kids to generalize and to make assumptions. Just as prejudice is a problem in society, it is a problem in our schools. The Voices of Experience were so vociferous about their concerns that the topic of prejudice just had to get its own chapter.

But don't be alarmed. These "vagrant opinions," voiced everywhere from the classroom to the cafeteria, tend to be more incidental than the work of degenerates. Kids say the darnedest things, and it is the teacher's job to set them straight. Prejudice becomes more serious, however, when it is an adult who is acting irresponsibly. This chapter focuses on all types of prejudice and how to effectively deal with each situation.

Dealing with Student-to-Student Prejudice

Students come in all shapes and sizes, and so, too, does their prejudice. On the bright side, the words they exchange are often meant to be harmless. On the not-so-bright side, rarely is a racist, sexist, or homophobe harmless. It's up to the teacher to turn these exchanges into teachable moments. Here are some Dos and Don'ts:

DO:

■ **Discuss the incident ASAP.** The students involved will have to be spoken to individually about the dangers of generalizations and of intentionally trying to hurt other people's feelings. If the whole class was witness, then you will want to address the issue with them as well.

■ **Allow the recipient of the prejudice to share her feelings.** Teachable moments always mean more when the message is being sent by a peer.

■ **Document the incident.** Many teachers have a three-ring binder with a section for each student. Include a page for "Incidents" as well as one for "Parent Contact." If situations get ugly, you'll be happy to have such evidence.

■ **Consider getting the parents and/or the administration involved.** At the least, they will have to be informed. Use your best judgment to determine when to get others involved and in what manner.

DON'T:

■ **Ignore the incident because you are too busy.** Small incidents can become big blowouts in a heartbeat!

■ **Treat the incident as if you are fighting the entire history of prejudice.** Keep in mind that these are kids experimenting with words and feelings. Don't go overboard, and don't forget to get to the heart of the matter (as quickly and concisely as possible). Oftentimes, racial epithets are used defensively.

■ **Be overly vocal in your sympathies for the "victim."** It's important to avoid, as best you can, focusing on the recipient, as these situations are usually hurtful and always embarrassing. Keep the instigator on the hot spot and keep the focus on his words and actions.

★ THE FACT OF THE MATTER ★

The five states with the highest numbers of hate crimes in 2002 were California, Massachusetts, Michigan, New Jersey, and New York. On the bright side, the FBI reported that the number of hate crimes decreased from a record-high 9,726 in 2001 to 7,462 in 2002 (a 23.3 percent decrease).

Source: "FBI Report Shows Decrease in Hate Crimes." Civilrights.org, 2003. http://www.civilrights.org/issues/hate/details.cfm?id=17044

Teach Your Children Well

Racism is a problem just like bullying; it comes overtly and subtly. It is a problem that requires immediate attention, like so many of the other nonacademic aspects of teaching.

THIRD-GRADE TEACHER, WHITE PLAINS, NY

I often tell my class that everyone is entitled to his beliefs but that when those beliefs are hurtful, they cannot be voiced in an offensive way and they cannot be voiced in my classroom. Discussion is one thing; being hurtful is another.

SCIENCE TEACHER, HIGGINSVILLE, MO

When something prejudicial has been said or done, I try and find a teacher or administrator representative of the "offended" category. Their words often have a greater impact on the student than mine.

FIFTH-GRADE TEACHER, ANNANDALE, VA

I take as much time as is needed to discuss differences in people. Usually, taking the time reveals deeper issues at work. All too often, students get their ideas from family. So we do a lot of conflict-resolution presentations.

KINDERGARTEN TEACHER, DETROIT, MI

When prejudice occurs in the classroom, you first need to empathize with both children involved and then help them empathize with each other. This is a teaching moment and should not be viewed as a discipline moment.

FIFTH-GRADE TEACHER, BERLIN, CT

Knowing that prejudice is going to be an issue every year, I try to head it off with a discussion the first week of school. That way, any time I have to deal with it, I can refer to the discussion.

SIXTH-GRADE TEACHER, BRONX, NY

Approaching the Problem Head On

It is important to me that we cherish our diversity and celebrate it as much as possible. I have had parents bring ethnic foods, clothing, and customs into my room. I also teach the children how to sing "Happy Birthday" in different languages.

THIRD-GRADE TEACHER, CHULA VISTA, CA

Although I never stray far, I often concoct a situation where two students with stereotypical thoughts about the other have to be in a room working together. They figure out pretty quickly that they aren't very different after all!

FIRST-GRADE TEACHER, COLORADO SPRINGS, CO

We had a new student start trouble with some of the special education students. Initially I tried talking to him, but it didn't work. The middle school was doing a project with several handicapped students, so we included this young man in the project. He came to like and respect them, and he didn't start any more trouble.

COMPUTER PROGRAMMING TEACHER, HEBRON, IN

Student-to-Teacher Prejudice

Angry words hurt; none more than personal affronts. There might be times when a student speaks prejudicially (and hurtfully) toward you. As with student-to-student issues, these incidents need to be turned into teachable moments. The following Dos and Don'ts might help:

DO:

■ **Give the student an opportunity to explain himself and to "backtrack" with dignity.** Still, make sure that his level of remorse is commensurate with the offense by not letting him off the hook too easily. Also, make sure that the discussion (tackling tough questions together) and repercussions (according to the discipline code) assure that this kind of thing never happens again.

■ **Document and report the incident.** As with student-to-student racism, you will want to cover yourself. Inform the parents of the incident, the discussion that ensued, and the consequence. If you send a note rather than phone home, have the parent sign off so *you know* that *they know.*

DON'T:

■ **Ignore the incident because it seems relatively harmless.** Don't let it go because you think "It's just a kid shootin' off her mouth." If it seems like it was no big deal for you, the student has no reason not to do it again to someone else.

■ **Forget to tell the student how you feel about what was said or done.** Your feelings are important—and can be what turns this into a real teachable moment!

teacher tip www.tolerance.org is a great website for learning how to promote tolerance in your classroom. Check it out!

Reacting Like an Educator

I tell the students that I'm offended by the use of certain words without naming those words. They're smart enough to know what those words are and smart enough to not use them.

KINDERGARTEN TEACHER, WHITE BEAR LAKE, MN

As a first-year teacher, I had a few students try to play the race card when I punished them for being disrespectful. I asked teachers who share the students' ethnicity to help me work with these kids, and they did. It ended up even better than I could have hoped.

PRE-ALGEBRA TEACHER, SENOIA, GA

"

I didn't expect an administrator to overreact when a special-needs student referred to me using a racial slur. I pointed out to the administrator that suspending the student would not teach him how to correct his attitude, since he didn't know he had done something wrong in the first place.

SPECIAL EDUCATION TEACHER, MALONE, NY

I dealt with a student yelling racial epithets at me by having "sensitivity sessions" with all my kids. Teaching tolerance is one of the most important things I do.

SPANISH TEACHER, TALLAHASSEE, FL

"

Prejudice from the Parents

There are just some situations that cannot be sugarcoated. When racism occurs between adults, especially when a parent acts prejudicially toward you, try to keep your cool and remember the following Dos and Don'ts:

DO:

- **Ask the parent to clarify.** There's always a chance that you misunderstood what he said. If you heard correctly, either ask the parent to leave your classroom or remove yourself; your immediate goal should be to avoid further conflict.

- **Inform an administrator.** Definitely, definitely, definitely inform an administrator! For your personal and professional protection, you don't want to wait until the situation escalates.

DON'T:

■ **Allow future conversations to veer away from the student's performance in your class.** Use the student's name repeatedly, as a subtle reminder, as well as the phrase "But what's important here . . ."

■ **Forget that actions, even more than words, can change people's minds.** Even adults can benefit from teachable moments. Prove yourself to this parent with everything from continued professionalism to your body language. Don't back down.

■ **Blame the child for his mother or father.** You only have to deal with this person on occasion; the child has to go home to the parent every day.

When Prejudice Is Directed at You: Age

A number of parents thought I was too young to be a good teacher. I told them that we needed to function as a team in order to present a united front so the child wouldn't attempt the "divide and conquer" strategy. By undermining me, due to age or anything else, that was liable to occur.

CHARACTER EDUCATION TEACHER, CHICAGO, IL

Parents are constantly judging me because of my age. One parent actually said to me, "You look like you would go out to a club all night and try to teach the next day." I stayed calm and described some of my qualifications. If you speak like a professional, eventually they realize you *are* a professional.

FIFTH-GRADE TEACHER, LAKE WORTH, FL

When Prejudice Is Directed at You: Race

I work in a school where I am in the minority. Bias and prejudice were daily occurrences until I proved myself . . . by being myself. You will have minimal problems once the parents see that you want the best for their child.

KINDERGARTEN TEACHER, SEVERNA PARK, MD

Cultural, racial, gender, and educational differences all come into play when you are working with parents. I found that the more respect the students had for me, the more respect their parents would have.

SPECIAL EDUCATION TEACHER, INDIANAPOLIS, IN

I have learned to show parents how important education and teamwork are, regardless of color or creed. Leading by example is always the best way. Stay productive and don't overreact!

ENGLISH AND JOURNALISM TEACHER, SUMMERTON, SC

I teach at a homogeneous private school, and one of the parents didn't think a teacher of a different color had any place at the school. I simply explained to her that I liked the school, I loved my students, and that I was there to help the students realize their potential. I also wanted to help prepare them for the real, integrated world.

FOURTH-GRADE TEACHER, IRVING, TX

Young children have a fresh and unspoiled outlook on the world—unfortunately, many times they emulate what they have been taught by their parents.

FIFTH-GRADE TEACHER, DANVILLE, VA

Many times parents of another race feel that you are giving their child a hard time because of race. A conference with parent and teacher makes a huge difference; talking face-to-face always helps.

SECOND-GRADE TEACHER, JOLIET, IL

Be Aware of Your Own Prejudices

Everybody passes judgment, has preconceived notions, and is inexperienced to varying degrees about what life is like for someone with a different background. If you are dedicated to working in a district with a diverse student population, then here are some of the things you can do to acclimate yourself and avoid potential problems:

DO:

■ **Act humbly.** This is not the time to act as if you know it all and have seen it all.

■ **Be open to the traditions of other cultures.** One of the benefits of working in such a school is getting to know about other people!

■ **Have conversations with students and parents about their cultural background.** Ask questions in a way that shows that you are eager to learn more about their way of life.

190

DON'T:

▪ **Make assumptions.** Even innocent assumptions are rarely correct.

▪ **Say things that might offend.** Even if you have faith in the student's ability "to take a joke," you are modeling behavior that you don't want to see in your students.

▪ **Work in a culturally diverse area unless you are curious about those other cultures (and willing to adapt to new customs).** Although it is a tricky balance to strike, part of being a successful teacher is being yourself while also immersing yourself.

▪ **Try and "convert" students and parents to your beliefs and traditions.** The goal is to teach them about others, just as you are learning about others. There is a difference between preaching and teaching. You are sure to hear it from parents and the principal if you overstep your boundaries.

teacher tip

Express your curiosity about other races and religions with questions and by attending cultural events. The Internet is also an excellent source of history and explanation for everything from Kwanzaa to Three Kings Day. By being able to answer someone else's questions, your interest will be made evident to all.

Fighting from the Inside Out

I try to really understand the values of the communities that I teach in. I understand that, although different, they are not better or worse. Having an understanding and appreciation for these differences is essential to being able to help the students.

READING SPECIALIST, CHICAGO, IL

It's important to know about the student and family. Socioeconomic status plays a part, as does generational poverty, in finding an approach to connect with people. In these cases, using "educationalese" usually does not bode well in conversations.

TEACHER LEADERSHIP INSTRUCTOR, OXFORD, OH

I would go to different community functions for my students of differing backgrounds and show my support. Eventually, they got used to having me around, and I was accepted.

SPECIAL EDUCATION TEACHER, SPRINGFIELD, VA

I made it a point to get to know my students' cultures and to show an interest in a variety of things that were special to them (i.e., music, food, etc.).

MATHEMATICS TEACHER, LYFORD, TX

Fighting the Good Fight with Books!

Here is a sampling of books that ably address prejudice without putting the kids to sleep. As further evidence, many of them have won the Newbery Award and/or the Coretta Scott King Author Award.

English teachers aren't the only ones who can expose kids to great literature, just as guidance counselors aren't the only educators able to guide them. Keeping that in mind, always preview material (for appropriateness, level of difficulty, etc.) before assigning it to your students.

FOR KINDERGARTEN THROUGH FOURTH-GRADE:

■ *The Crayon Box that Talked* by Michael Letzig and Shane Derolf

■ *Autumn Street* by Lois Lowry

■ *Baseball Saved Us* by Ken Mochizuki

■ *Maniac Magee* by Jerry Spinelli

FOR FIFTH THROUGH EIGHTH GRADES

(Of the three age groups, this is the most important for dealing with prejudice, as students are really beginning to come to terms with this concept):

- *The Watsons Go to Birmingham–1963* by Christopher Paul Curtis
- *The Breadwinner* by Deborah Ellis
- *Monster* by Walter Dean Myers
- *My Name Is Not Angelica* by Scott O'Dell
- *Holes* by Louis Sachar
- *The Star Fisher* by Laurence Yep
- Anything written by Mildred Taylor

FOR NINTH THROUGH TWELFTH GRADES:

- *Liberty Circle* by Phil Campagna

- *Black Like Me* by John Howard Griffin

- *Bronx Masquerade* by Nikki Grimes

- *To Kill a Mockingbird* by Harper Lee

- *Night* by Elie Wiesel

- *Native Son* by Richard A. Wright

Dealing with Prejudice

Tolerance is probably the most important thing that we teach our students. It is also an area in which teachers can really prove themselves and show growth. Dealing with prejudice is just one of the many ways you will improve yourself as a teacher (and a person). In the next chapter, the Voices of Experience discuss a number of other ways in which you can develop as a professional.

CHAPTER 8

Professional Growth

"I always assumed that my education would end after college. Nothing could be further from the truth!

English teacher, Summit, NJ

Part of the human condition is change, and the more you can do to encourage positive change for yourself, the better. This includes everything from working with a mentor to furthering your education—the former being a want and the latter being a need if you are to maintain your certification. Professional growth comes in many ways; sometimes it will seek you out, but most of the time you have to be the seeker. This chapter will show you how to hunt down and make the most of those opportunities.

A Mentor Makes All the Difference

Why is having a mentor so important during your first year as a teacher? You're probably thinking that you can just ask around if you need help with something—why be assigned to one particular person? Well, a book of a thousand pages *might* allow description for all the ways in which an official (i.e., paid and accountable) mentor can be of help, but the top-ten list below is a good start. Having a mentor is like one-stop shopping for all of the following. A mentor will:

1. Serve as your own personal tour guide around the building and district.

2. Provide helpful reminders regarding important dates (for example, when midterm notices are due).

3. Help build your confidence with well-timed praise and, more importantly, by showing you how the slightest of adjustments can make a huge difference in your teaching.

4. Be the "A" in your Q&A! Mentors are there for you to ask as many questions as you want. They will provide answers and advice on essentials like classroom management and lesson planning.

5. Run through a mock observation and evaluation with you, as well as let you know the kinds of categories included on the observation form.

6. Serve as your advocate with administrators and colleagues; even with parents and students, if necessary.

7. Interpret curriculum, memos, and the legal mumbo jumbo.

8. Play junior psychologist for all of your worries.

9. Describe procedures for things like fire drills, assemblies, lunch duty, and requesting a bus for a field trip.

10. Show you what forms you need and how to fill them out; this can benefit you personally (personal-day request) and professionally (work orders, etc.).

And, unlike all of the other helpful folks around the building, you mentor will *always* be there for you, day or night.

★ THE FACT OF THE MATTER ★

More than half the states in the country now require mentoring for entry-level teachers.

Source: Sharon Feiman-Nemser. Teacher Mentoring: A Critical Review. ERIC Clearinghouse on Teaching and Teacher Education, 1998. http://www.nfie.org/publications/mentoring.htm

A Great, Great Help

My mentor taught me how to discipline with dignity and to teach successfully through planning, assessing, and making the lessons interesting. LANGUAGE ARTS TEACHER, DEL RIO, TX

A qualified mentor can be instrumental in figuring out your strengths and weaknesses. Then she can help strengthen those weak areas. HISTORY AND LITERATURE TEACHER, TUCSON, AZ

More often than not, a mentor can mean the difference between an awful first year and one that is bearable. Without their guidance, we'd all be lost! KINDERGARTEN TEACHER, IOWA CITY, IA

I'll never forget my mentor. We were friends, but in some ways, I was like one of her students, too.

CURRICULUM SPECIALIST, ARMONK, NY

I had three mentors my first year: a third grade teacher (my official mentor), the principal's secretary, and a paraprofessional who'd been in the school for 17 years. From each, I learned tons!

SECOND-GRADE TEACHER, WORCESTER, MA

Finding the Right Match

Hopefully, your supervisor will be able to assign you a mentor soon after you're hired. However, this isn't always the case—sometimes new teachers have to find their own mentor, official or otherwise. To ensure that you get someone to work with who will be a good match for you, here are some steps to follow:

■ **Bug your supervisor.** Don't be afraid to ask again and again if you don't get a response. This is important!

■ **Talk to other teachers at staff meetings and workshops.** Feel out the situation to see who might be willing to help. If you join a professional organization, you might even find someone from a different district to mentor you.

■ **Try your best to find a mentor in your subject area.** While any teacher can help you learn classroom management, only a teacher with a similar expertise can help you to teach your particular subject and grade level.

■ **Determine how much experience you would like your mentor to have.** Should your mentor be a relatively new teacher or someone who has been teaching for many years? There are pros and cons to both: experience versus energy, knowledge versus shared experience, maternal or paternal support versus a buddy to hang with. Of course, these pros and cons aren't sealed in stone, as every district has at least one Energizer Bunny of a mentor who's going back for her third master's degree despite being a grandmother!

■ **Focus on convenience, if possible.** Do you and your mentor have a similar schedule (same prep periods free, for example)? Is your mentor's classroom close enough for quick Q&A as well as observations (you observing him and vice-versa)? Do you both arrive early? Stay late? Eat lunch in the staff lounge? The more alike your work habits, the more available your mentor will be.

Being Proactive

If it's November and you still don't have a mentor, start giving your principal subtle reminders. It is well worth the effort.

FRENCH TEACHER, MONTAUK, NY

Finding an exceptionally talented teacher who can serve as a mentor is the single most important thing a newbie can do to make that first year a success. The hope is that you will find someone who teaches the same subjects, but if not, just be happy to have the help.

THIRD-GRADE TEACHER, ANNISTON, AL

Find another teacher to confide in, one who can explain the politics and how to "work smart" as opposed to just working hard. The principal should help you in finding this mentor—even if the person is an "unofficial" mentor.

ENGLISH TEACHER, SAN DIEGO, CA

207

Getting Your Master's Degree

Although it's safe to say that almost 100 percent of teachers will obtain a master's degree, the Voices of Experience offer a variety of advice as to *when* it is best to go back to school. There are benefits to getting started right away, just as there are drawbacks. The same can be said of waiting a few years (just beware the ills of procrastination!). Whatever the window of opportunity, here's what you should know about the process:

■ Although the details vary from state to state, for the most part, all teachers *must* earn their master's degree within five years of entering the classroom. If you do not complete this work, your school has to apply for an emergency variance to keep you on.

■ In most graduate school programs, you will have to complete 36 credits, including a term of student teaching, to receive your master's. Graduation is also dependent on the completion of a project, thesis, or test at the end of your studies.

- Find a program that fits your schedule and be diligent about setting aside time not only for class but for homework. Ask yourself how many classes you can handle at one time. Would you be better off taking classes after work or on weekends?

- Consider going back for a dual certification (e.g., a special education certification to complement your elementary education certification, math certification to complement your science certification, etc.). It will increase your attractiveness during the hiring process and will make you a more knowledgeable teacher.

    Author's note: So much of what I learned while earning my master's in special education applies to teaching in general. I highly recommend a few special education classes, if not the whole degree!

- In most districts, you can get tuition reimbursement (a small percentage), and your salary may increase with each class (three credits) completed, just as it may increase significantly once you get your degree. Check your union contract for the details, and be sure to keep all documentation and to copy it for the payroll department.

■ If you live in a remote area of the country or don't have time to travel to a classroom, perhaps an online university is the thing for you. Distance learning programs have grown in popularity as the Internet has grown in popularity. Just make sure the university is an accredited institution and that your district and state will accept the degree before mailing in the first check!

■ Ask other new teachers in your school if they'd like to take classes with you. It's always more fun to have a partner in crime!

teacher tip Oftentimes your regular teaching can qualify as your student teaching requirement for graduate school. Check with your advisor and/or the professor in charge of supervising student teachers to see if this is the case.

Start as Soon as Possible

Start with a class per semester and then load up during the summer. Ongoing learning is best when you are highly motivated.

SECOND-GRADE TEACHER, WASHINGTON, DC

Going back to school early in your career will help better prepare you for teaching, and it will maximize your earning potential.

THIRD-GRADE TEACHER, NORTH CALDWELL, NJ

During the initial years of teaching, the master's program can provide a real support network. Just be sure to find a program that doesn't interfere with your other responsibilities.

THIRD-GRADE TEACHER, CHULA VISTA, CA

Wait Till You Know What You Want

Use that first year to develop a teaching rhythm and to adjust to the intensive demands of the career. Once you feel comfortable with your teaching assignment, then and only then should you go for that degree.

ENGLISH TEACHER, SUMMERTON, SC

The best time to get your master's is after at least three years of teaching. The background knowledge will allow you to bring so much more to the master's program, and thus you will gain so much more from your degree.

READING SPECIALIST, VANCOUVER, WA

Start slow with a degree. Be sure that you have chosen a field in which you are truly interested rather than simply working toward a degree for the money.

FIFTH-GRADE TEACHER, ANNANDALE, VA

Teachers need to continually take courses, attend professional development workshops, read articles, and conduct research. When we think of a master's degree as an end point, we lose sight of the idea of being a lifelong learner.

MATHEMATICS TEACHER, PENFIELD, NY

213

Conferences and Committees

Opportunities for professional development sessions and themed conferences will present themselves throughout the school year, and as long as you can attend without falling too far behind in your lessons, you should definitely take advantage of them. Like a master's program, these "classes" are often a way to keep up with the latest and greatest in curriculum. They are also a good way to recharge your batteries; there's nothing wrong with a day away from the kiddies and the chance to eat a civil lunch with your peers!

Here are a few things you should know about attending these types of events:

■ Find out if your district does a lot of its own "in-house" professional development and how you can participate. (There will be plenty of flyers and pamphlets in your box.) These don't cost anything to attend and are usually very informative.

■ The less expensive the fee is for a conference, the more likely you are to receive approval to attend.

■ Usually, you will have to submit the request a few weeks in advance of the conference date. Leave plenty of time to get approval and to make your plans.

■ Summer vacations are a great time to attend a two- or three-day conference in your subject area.

■ Conferences not only teach you about your subject matter but introduce you to other teachers, methods, and products available for classroom use in that field.

Attending Is Well Worth It!

Every once in a while, it's good to step outside of the seclusion of your room. There's a whole world out there, and every day teachers are learning from one another.

STAFF DEVELOPER, MENDOCINO, CA

I learned as much from the district's in-services as I did in grad school! From phonics to dealing with bullying, these half-day sessions were great. **FIRST-GRADE TEACHER, NEW HAVEN, CT**

As much as we all love our students, to have a day away is nice. Teachers can eat lunch together, exchange ideas and phone numbers, and learn how other schools are going about trying to build the better mousetrap.

MATHEMATICS TEACHER, ST. LOUIS, MO

Rarely do I think a professional development day is not worth it. There is a lot of research going on out there, and it's hard to keep up on your own. **SOCIAL STUDIES TEACHER, HELENA, MT**

Lending a Hand

Schools are dynamic institutions, and in order for them to thrive, everybody has to pitch in well above and beyond the call of duty. Kids learn as much out of the classroom as within, and the same can be said of teachers. Below is a list of potential opportunities for you to help.

■ **Committees:** Earth Day, technology, field trips, graduation, Hispanic Heritage Day, and so on all require committees, endless committees! There's always something to help plan.
On the flip side: Committees also happen to be the best way to learn how your school is run and how to get things done.

■ **Coaching:** Whatever the sport, coaching *always* takes more time than you think.
On the flip side: It's a fantastic way to get to know the kids better—and their parents, too!

■ **Club advisor:** Serving in this capacity is not a huge time and energy drain, but you will have a lot you want to do after school, and this will just add to the list.

On the flip side: Extracurricular activities often motivate the students to do well in school and also to behave. Without advisors, there can be no clubs.

■ **Tutoring:** Offering extra help after school is fine, but be careful about taking on too many students on an individual basis.

On the flip side: Individual help is often the boost that students need to succeed.

- **School events:** Attending and even chaperoning is nice, and you will want to show that you care, but check your calendar before agreeing. If you wanted to do something that Friday night and have already said yes to the student council . . . bye-bye, Friday night!

On the flip side: It's awesome to see the kids interact outside of the classroom. Plus, you might even have a little bit of fun yourself!

teacher tip

Just be careful how often you say yes. The most important thing during the first 100 days is that you become the best teacher you can possibly be. You will always feel somewhat selfish when you say no, especially if it's to a student. It's okay to say no, though. Just explain a little and make a mental note to say yes the next time.

Volunteering

Nobody knows how busy you are, so they won't hesitate to ask for your help. Be very wise about what you agree to. You don't want to agree and then give less than 100 percent.

EARTH SCIENCE TEACHER, WHITE PLAINS, NY

Coaching intramurals was a good opportunity to get to know kids not in my classes.

SOCIAL STUDIES TEACHER, CHARLESTON, SC

Sometimes I feel like half the job of teaching involves volunteering your time. Whether it's relationship-building with the kids or simply making your school a happier place where behavior is not a problem, putting together opportunities for the students is usually well worth it.

THIRD-GRADE TEACHER, EL CAMINO, NM

Creating a Personal Mission Statement

With all these options for professional growth, you might feel overwhelmed. Don't lose sight of your plan of action, let alone your personal philosophy. A Voice of Experience from Brighton, Massachusetts, sent in a wonderful suggestion, the kind of thing you are rarely told about in education classes:

> *"Write yourself a mission statement. Hang one copy by the door of your classroom. Hang one copy by your bathroom mirror. And hang one copy on your refrigerator. Revise this statement as it begins to wear thin and as you identify new goals that you'd like to be reminded of. Don't worry if you don't feel like making any changes for a long time, or if you make changes every day for a month. Learning, like love, does not stick to a schedule! Finally, keep the old copies as signs of your personal growth."*

Teachers are indeed lifelong learners.

Someday soon you will be a Voice of Experience to some other lucky teacher. But if you're to ever reach that point, it's essential that you remain happy with your career choice and comfortable with your financial future. Set goals and plan well and this is sure to be the case. The next chapter will provide you with the resources to do so.

9

Organizations and Resources

"
I wouldn't be quite so professional if not for the professional organizations that I belong to!

Social studies teacher, Santa Fe, NM

"

There are many organizations and resources out there designed specifically to help you in your quest for professional growth. From unions to associations to local grant-giving foundations, these folks—usually part of a nonprofit initiative—are professionals willing to share their experiences (and sometimes their dollars!). Ask a teacher in your subject area or grade level what professional organizations he belongs to. Surf the Internet for descriptions and contact information, and seek out professors past (undergrad) and present (grad) for their advice; chances are, they already belong and can point you down the right path. This chapter will get you started!

Keep Up with Your Reading

There are countless magazines and journals, all with a focus on education. Time being the scarce resource that it is, subscribe to one publication that's specific to your field, and take the time to read an article per week from one of the general publications that you'll probably find in the teachers' lounge at school. Although the Internet has made finding answers to specific questions much, much easier, there is still something to be said for keeping up with the industry by embracing the printed word.

The following is a list of recommended publications that fall under that "general" category:

- *American Educator*
- *Harvard Educational Review*
- *The New York Times* "Education Life"
- The *Phi Delta Kappan*

teacher tip As far as publications and research go, there is also the ubiquitous Internet. Education World (www.educationworld.com) has something for everyone and is highly, highly recommended!

Reading Is Fundamental

Although I still fit in some pleasure reading during my first year, I found myself reading and enjoying curriculum-related materials, especially the latest news.

SCIENCE TEACHER, MONTGOMERY, AL

I always make it a point to be up on not just curriculum but also current events—politics, sports, the weather, everything. Even though I'm bone-tired at the end of the day, I want to be able to engage students in these kinds of conversations.

SPANISH TEACHER, KANSAS CITY, MO

Fortunately, I was able to find the *Phi Delta Kappan* and *American Educator* in our staff lounge. The time it takes to flip through these is well worth it. I usually run across something to share with my fellow teachers as well as lessons to try with my kids.

FIFTH-GRADE TEACHER, SPOKANE, WA

Professional Organizations

Joining a professional organization has many benefits. Although it is yet another item added to your already jam-packed schedule and another expense to your already stretched-thin budget, you will find that participating is well worth the time and membership dues. And, like the expense, the time required is not great; usually no more than two or three hours per month. A small price to pay, especially when compared to all you will learn.

Still not convinced? Read on to learn more.

■ Being informed means you are meeting one of the tenets of "professional responsibility." Relevant information will be shared at meetings and conferences, and you will notice, in ways big and small, how knowing these things will have a positive impact on your teaching and on how you present yourself to colleagues and parents.

■ You'll get to know others in your subject area. This allows for the exchange of ideas and also substantial networking opportunities. Many a teacher has ended up at a different, preferable school as a result of attending such meetings!

■ Oftentimes, these councils and associations use local universities for their meetings, so attending might help you decide where you want to apply to graduate school.

■ Membership sure looks good on a résumé.

The Right One for You

Not sure where to begin looking for professional organizations to join? Here's a list of some of the largest organizations out there. There's something on this list for everybody!

- **The Council for Exceptional Children (CEC).**
  This organization is for the special education teacher or the regular education teacher who wants to learn more about his or her classified students. Also recommended for the teacher who is considering a master's degree in special education.
  www.cec.sped.org

- **International Reading Association (IRA).**
  The foundation of all education is the ability to read.
  www.reading.org

■ **National Association for the Education of Young Children (NAEYC).**

If you work with kids in the primary grades, this could benefit you.

www.naeyc.org

■ **National Council of Social Studies (NCSS).**

This council addresses social studies education at *all* grade levels.

www.ncss.org

■ **National Council of Teachers of English (NCTE).**

This is the nation's top professional organization for English teachers.

www.ncte.org

■ **National Council of Teachers of Mathematics (NCTM).**

This is the nation's top professional organization for math teachers.

www.nctm.org

■ **National Middle School Association (NMSA).**

The NMSA deals with those awkward, in-between years. If you teach sixth, seventh, or eighth grade, you need this kind of help!

www.nmsa.org

■ **National Science Teachers Association (NSTA).**

One of the most highly regarded professional organizations, the NSTA has its hand in all things science.

www.nsta.org

■ **Teachers of English to Speakers of Other Languages (TESOL).**

Given the changing face of our student population, the work of TESOL has become more important than ever before.

www.tesol.edu

Professional Behavior

I highly recommend joining a professional organization or two and reading their literature about everything from the developmental stages of children to proposed teaching legislation. It's so easy to get caught up in managing your classroom, and meanwhile, there's so much else going on in the teaching world that you don't know about.

FIFTH-GRADE TEACHER, JOHNSON CITY, TN

There are professional organizations for every field and subject, and it doesn't hurt to keep up-to-date.

EARLY READING SUCCESS TEACHER, WEST HAVEN, CT

The information I have become privy to and the contacts I've made by joining professional organizations have been phenomenal!

SPECIAL EDUCATION TEACHER, TARRYTOWN, NY

Unions

Among the many unsung heroes in public education are your district-level union leaders. They work to bring professional development opportunities to the staff and are also the folks you'll turn to if you need to file a grievance. Nationally, union leadership has shown, time and time again, a willingness to fight not just for America's teachers but for America's children. Here are some of the specific benefits of joining a union:

■ **Their credit unions usually have very good rates.**

They offer savings and checking accounts (sometimes at no fee).

Car and home loans are available at exceptionally low rates.

Direct deposit can be arranged so that your paycheck goes into your account on Thursday night.

■ **They offer legal representation.**

If a lawsuit involving a student or parent should arise, the union will provide you with legal representation. They will negotiate your salary and health benefits on your behalf when your contract runs out.

■ **You'll get special deals in a number of areas.**

Outside agencies (e.g., travel agencies, fast food restaurants, theme parks) will make offers to union members; the larger the union, the more offers that will be made available (collective buying power!). Some school districts do not offer dental benefits; if this is the case, usually the union will have a plan or two available.

DEFINING A "GRIEVANCE": A "grievance" is a complaint filed by an employee or union member in regards to a violation committed against him (e.g., an administrator conducts an official observation without advance notice and a preobservation conference). The union has a grievance chairperson who meets with the school's administrators to resolve the issue. As with any legal proceeding, the matter is supposed to be addressed in a speedy manner. If no resolution can be reached, an arbitrator may be called in to mediate.

Joining the Union

In most districts, you can either join the union or opt out and only pay partial dues. (This is required because of labor laws.) Usually, union dues are deducted from your paycheck once a month. By the end of the year, something in the neighborhood of $400 will have gone toward the union. Plan accordingly, and don't be afraid to ask union leaders where your hard-earned money is going.

Also of note: At least once a year, you will probably be asked to donate to a lobbying group that works at the state and possibly even the federal level. These political action committees (PACs) look out for teachers and schools by gently reminding legislators how they should vote on the issues that affect schools, teachers, and children. Here are some of the major national unions that you may end up affiliated with:

■ **National Education Association (NEA):** Founded in 1857, the NEA is headquartered in Washington, D.C. Its members "work at every level of education, from preschool to university graduate programs." Although this organization, close to three million strong, does not tout itself as a "union," the NEA often functions in that role.

Source: www.nea.org

■ **American Federation of Teachers (AFT):** Also headquartered in Washington, D.C., the AFT helped pioneer the collective bargaining approach to negotiation. By not limiting itself to just public school teachers, the AFT has grown to more than one million members.

Source: www.aft.org

■ **The National Education Association and American Federation of Teachers (NEAFT):** This partnership began in 2000. Each organization is still free to conduct its work independently and to even disagree with each other on educational issues. However, in addressing together as many issues as possible, their strengths and influence can be maximized. The NEAFT partnership works to address "critical educational issues and issues of vital significance to children."

Source: www.aft.org/neaft

 *teacher tip*

There will be a big, well-advertised union meeting at the beginning of the school year. You will also find lots of small freebies (pencils, notepads, calendars) left in your box. Go to the meeting with an open mind and see what you think!

In Favor of Membership

Unions are a vital necessity in the education world, where administrators are trained educators but not necessarily trained managers. Your principal might not know what she can legally ask of you. The grievance chairperson and the assistant superintendent in charge of grievances are probably the only two in the district who really know.

SOCIAL STUDIES TEACHER, IOWA CITY, IA

You don't miss the water till the wells run dry and you don't know how much you need your union till the proverbial poop hits the fan!

THIRD-GRADE TEACHER, LOS ANGELES, CA

"

Teachers are often threatened by political rhetoric, especially during an election year and especially when the state is running a massive debt. My first experience with this was quite the reality check. Good thing the union fought for us in the press and in the legislature, otherwise I might have lost my job. Untenured teachers are the first to go.

KINDERGARTEN TEACHER, BATAVIA, NY

Union conferences are a great way to recharge the batteries. Meeting colleagues from around the country and learning about cutting-edge initiatives will get any teacher excited!

ENGLISH TEACHER, PITTSFIELD, MA

"

Grants, Grants Everywhere!

One way that some organizations lend a hand is by offering grant money. Sometime after Halloween (administrators like to have their budgets set by January 1), begin sniffing around to see what you might be able to get for the following school year. It's amazing how helpful a few hundred dollars can be! Here are some options:

- **Minigrants:** These are usually $1,000 or less and are offered by organizations and foundations. Be on the lookout for flyers in the staff lounge that will tell you how to apply.

- **School board grants:** These are small amounts of money (usually less than $1,000) and are offered by the board of education; sniff these out in much the same manner as the aforementioned minigrants.

■ **Corporate grants:** These offer more money than minigrants, usually for yearlong projects in a specific area of study. An Internet search will help you find examples of these. Type in *grant, money, funds,* and your subject area or grade level to locate them.

One example of a corporate grant is the Toyota Tapestry (www.nsta.org/programs/tapestry). It's in conjunction with the National Science Teachers Association and offers grants ranging from $2,500 to $10,000 to K–12 science teachers for innovative projects.

■ **Corporate awards/recognition:** The school of a nominated teacher is granted money; an Internet search like the one described above will reveal these opportunities, especially if you also type in *awards.* If you have someone in mind, nominate her. And who knows, maybe someday you, too will be nominated!

One example of a corporate award is the Phi Delta Kappa Wal-Mart Teacher of the Year award (www.pdkintl.org/walmart/home.htm). There is a simple, printable application available online.

◆ $1,000 grants are given to hundreds of teachers. These awardees can then apply to be the state's leading teacher, with a $10,000 check going to the winner's school. The 50 winners then hope to be chosen as National Teacher of the Year, because this means an additional $25,000 for the school (a total of $36,000 for your school means you probably won't have to serve bus duty any time soon!).

■ **National foundation grants:** These work in the same way a corporate grant does and can be found through the same search engines.

One example of a national foundation grant is the National Education Association Foundation for the Improvement of Education, or NFIE (www.nfie.org/grants.htm). This grant is awarded to individuals and groups of teachers and ranges from $2,000 to $5,000.

■ **Government grants:** These include large sums of money offered by a particular government department for work in a particular area of study (ditto on the Internet search).

One example of a government grant is money awarded by the Environmental Protection Agency (www.epa.gov/epahome/grants.htm) in recognition of projects that enhance the public's awareness, knowledge, and skills in areas of environmental education.

■ **Citizen philanthropy grants:** This is a new means of applying for funds. Impress the philanthropists and watch the money roll in!

One place to find this kind of grant is through Donors Choose (http://www.donorchoose.org), where teachers list their proposals and the donors decide what project they would like to fund. This opportunity is currently available only in New York and North Carolina.

Don't Take 'Em for Granted

Many granting organizations conduct a workshop on filling out their application. Definitely attend—it will increase your chances of obtaining the grant. Also, deadlines are non-negotiable, so be sure to send everything in on time!

THIRD- THROUGH FIFTH-GRADE TEACHER, BROOKLYN, NY

I was pleasantly surprised the first time I was awarded a grant. It's amazing how even $500 helps.

SCIENCE TEACHER, SANTA MONICA, CA

Grant boards aren't interested in spending time on incomplete applications, so they usually make their guidelines very clear. Don't be afraid to find out who's on the board, either. If you happen to know someone on a board, there's no harm in contacting that person.

FIFTH-GRADE TEACHER, LAS VEGAS, NV

Getting a grant was one of the best things to ever happen to me as a teacher. The money obviously added to my classroom, but one benefit I hadn't anticipated was how the accountability requirements made me a better teacher. By having to report the results, I really thought about what we'd accomplished and what the kids had learned.

SECOND-GRADE TEACHER, IOWA CITY, IA

The preceding chapters hopefully helped you with your growth inside and outside the classroom. Now, the Voices of Experience want to leave you with some lighthearted words of wisdom. Best of luck in your teaching, and always remember why you walked into the classroom in the first place: it's all for the kids.

10

Final Words of Wisdom

> **If I win the lottery, I'll still teach.**
>
> *English teacher, Belleair, FL*

This final chapter is one last chance for the Voices of Experience to share their advice with you, the rookie, the newbie, the protégé, the future mentor and master teacher! Just as closure is a necessary component of any good lesson plan, no book on teaching would be complete without it. "Final Words of Wisdom" is this closure, delivered right before the bell rings.

Create Your Own Style

There is no secret recipe for being a good teacher. It's all trial and error, so keep trying until it works—and then try to make it better!

MAGNET COORDINATOR, NEW HAVEN, CT

Take the advice of others, but mold it to fit you.

FIRST-GRADE TEACHER, GRANBURY, TX

Listen to advice, read great professional books and journals, but always weigh the information against your own philosophy of teaching, and do what is right for the kids.

FIFTH-GRADE TEACHER, BERLIN, CT

"
Don't let the calendar drive the curriculum. Take the time to follow the path of your students' curiosity.

CURRICULUM DIRECTOR, SCARSDALE, NY

You'll want to leave plenty of room on the walls for student work, but don't miss the opportunity to let the students get to know you: postcards are a great conversation starter, as is indigenous art.

SPANISH TEACHER, FAIR LAWN, NJ

If you are truly a kind person, be <u>that</u> person in your classroom. Don't look to the disciplinarian down the hall and try to be like her.

MATHEMATICS TEACHER, NORTH CHICAGO, IL

Make sure that you enjoy kids enough to give them your heart, because most of the time they will either fill it with joy or break it with disappointment.

ENGLISH AND BUSINESS TEACHER, HAMLIN, WV

Persistence is the key. When reality sets in, a clear vision of what you want to accomplish for yourself and for the kids is vital.

INSTRUMENTAL MUSIC TEACHER, GAINESVILLE, GA

Dress up, tell jokes, wear crazy hats, tell interesting stories, and thrill them with your subject in a way they've never experienced.

HISTORY AND LITERATURE TEACHER, TUCSON, AZ

Learn from Your Students

Kids have open minds, open hearts, and are willing to share their thoughts and opinions if you'll let them.

SPECIAL EDUCATION TEACHER, WHITE BEAR LAKE, MN

The students have shown me that sometimes I need to relax and hand over the reins. They run a pretty good class when given the opportunity! **WORLD AND AMERICAN LITERATURE TEACHER, HOUSTON, TX**

Who better to teach you about the future, let alone different religions, cultures, and traditions, than your very own students. Tap that resource! **THIRD-GRADE TEACHER, ROME, NY**

★ THE FACT OF THE MATTER ★

Sixty percent of teachers surveyed said that they would return to teaching if they had the opportunity to start all over again. The main reason they would do this: "the desire to work with young people."

Source: "Status of the American Public School Teacher: 2000-2001." National Education Association. 2003. http://www.nea.org/edstats/images/status.pdf.

The students have taught me how to think outside the box. They always amaze me with logical answers that I haven't thought of.

THIRD-GRADE TEACHER, BRADENTON, FL

My students have taught me to avoid making assumptions.

CHARACTER EDUCATION TEACHER, CHICAGO, IL

Despite their age, kids are wise, forgiving, and have an immense capacity to love. Sometimes they're role models for *us!*

SECOND-GRADE TEACHER, CENTRAL ISLIP, NY

Avoid Common Pitfalls

No two students are alike, even if they come from the same family or have the same "label."

SPEECH AND LANGUAGE THERAPIST, ALBUQUERQUE, NM

Distinguish between not liking the behavior and not liking the child.

SECOND-GRADE TEACHER, SINGAPORE

Don't try to be their friend. They have lots of those. Be their mentor.

SECOND-GRADE TEACHER, MONTPELIER, VT

To the best of your ability, welcome the parents into your room. Get them involved in their child's education as well as in the school.

FOURTH-GRADE TEACHER, NEW HAVEN, CT

Always praise in public and reprimand in private.

READING TEACHER, STATEN ISLAND, NY

Keep in mind that school is a place for them to use their pencils but also their erasers. Let them make mistakes, and then show them how to correct the mistakes.

SPECIAL EDUCATION TEACHER, POWAY, CA

Procrastinating on your paperwork is a dangerous mistake guaranteed to come back and bite you!

SCIENCE TEACHER, PHILADELPHIA, PA

253

Don't Judge a Book by Its Cover

Teenagers will tell you that they do not care, but they do care—about themselves, others, the world, and many other important issues surrounding them.

BUSINESS TEACHER, BALTIMORE, MD

They're tired of being treated as kids and will appreciate the chance to show you how mature they are.

EIGHTH-GRADE TEACHER, PORT CHESTER, NY

Kids don't want to be bad. If they're acting out, there's a reason. Try to build up a relationship and give that child positive attention. You might find that this will be your favorite student by the end of the year.

VOCATIONAL STUDIES TEACHER, OWENSBORO, KY

Those students that are the hardest to love need love the most.

KINDERGARTEN THROUGH SECOND-GRADE TEACHER, CHATEAUGAY, NY

One can never make a decision on who will succeed and who will not. Some of the most promising students have wasted their abilities, while some of the most challenged students have been the most successful.

PHYSICAL SCIENCE TEACHER, EL CAJON, CA

If you challenge students, they *will* live up to your expectations.

SCIENCE TEACHER, HIGGINSVILLE, MO

If you can be open and accommodating to kids, then you can be open and accommodating to your coworkers as well.

SECOND-GRADE TEACHER, PROVIDENCE, RI

255

Do Unto Others . . .

If you have genuine enthusiasm for your subject and for your kids, they will have enthusiasm for what you're teaching them.

MATHEMATICS TEACHER, PENFIELD, NY

Put yourself in your students' shoes before you make decisions.

COMPUTER APPLICATIONS TEACHER, MITCHELL, SD

Make them feel as though what they're doing is important, and they'll believe that it is!

LANGUAGE ARTS AND SOCIAL STUDIES TEACHER, SAN FRANCISCO, CA

Practice what you preach. If you want the students to give their best, you should give your best, too. Be a model for what you expect.

ENGLISH TEACHER, SALEM, NC

Always remember that you're not the only adult in the building privy to good days and bad. Check in on your coworkers every once in a while.

SPECIAL EDUCATION TEACHER, MADISON, CT

Go the Extra Mile

Get involved in the school community. Kids love you when they know that you are willing to invest in them; it is one thing that they really don't believe adults want to do. Learn to relate and try to act spontaneously. It keeps them guessing!

EARTH SCIENCE TEACHER, CAVE CREEK, AZ

Be prepared for long evenings of paperwork. The efforts you make, especially at the beginning of the year, will pay off in the end. **KINDERGARTEN TEACHER, BRADENTON, FL**

Avoid burnout by adding more fuel. You need to keep learning throughout your career!

MATHEMATICS TEACHER, ST. PAUL, MN

Someone once told me that being a good teacher is really hard and being a bad teacher is really easy. I've never forgotten that and am still striving to be better.

SOCIAL STUDIES TEACHER, KANSAS CITY, MO

Stay Positive

Sarcasm has no place in a school at the student or administrative level.

SCIENCE TEACHER, HOUSTON, TX

Students don't hold grudges. Their memories are short and they can bounce back from just about anything. You should learn how to bounce back as well.

ENGLISH AND AMERICAN HISTORY TEACHER, OAKLAND, CA

Praise and encouragement go a long, long way.

SPEECH AND LANGUAGE THERAPIST, CHAMPAIGN, IL

Take Time to Enjoy the Perks

How many adults can say they have their summers off?

ENGLISH TEACHER, GALVESTON, TX

I find so many sympathetic, supportive people who appreciate teachers: in the grocery store, at parties, in my family, everywhere. It's definitely different from when I first started. Some businesses even give us discounts!

FIRST-GRADE TEACHER, GENEVA, NY

Tutoring is a great way to supplement your income. You can even do it from home.

LANGUAGE ARTS TEACHER, BOULDER, CO

On those days that you need to be at the dentist's office by three or to pick your child up from school, you can do it. The day-to-day schedule really is nice.

THIRD-GRADE TEACHER, BETHEL, ME

Each year I spend with the kids, I feel younger. A nice perk, indeed!

FIFTH-GRADE TEACHER, BROOKLYN, NY

Hang In There!

It really does all come together in the end.

SPECIAL EDUCATION TEACHER, HARRISBURG, PA

I learned that the process is often more valuable than the product. Don't just focus on the test score!

SPECIAL EDUCATION TEACHER, CAMBRIDGE, MA

It gets easier, but September is always nuts. Even after 15 years!

FOURTH-GRADE TEACHER, RANCHO SANTA FE, CA

Keep at it. It's hard at first but well worth the time and frustration. Besides, the kids need us!

SPECIAL EDUCATION TEACHER FOR THE VISUALLY IMPAIRED, CHARLESTON, SC

You *can* make a difference, one kid at a time.

ENGLISH TEACHER, PIPESTONE, MN

Conclusion: The ABC's of Success

Teachers experience so many highs and lows. One day the roller coaster that is your classroom will peak, the next day you'll be careening back down at breakneck speeds, screaming at the top of your lungs. But through it all, just as you will appreciate the help of veteran teachers, your students will appreciate your love, concern, and desire to help them learn. Empathy is the most important attribute a teacher can have, and guess what? You definitely have it. You already cared enough to set foot in the classroom. You cared enough to read this entire book!

The most important thing to remember is that you can and will be a competent educator. Every experienced teacher has had that moment of realization: "Hey, you know what? I *am* good at this!" On the next few pages, you'll find their A-to-Z's of success. Some day soon you'll find yours, too. Best of luck!

All that I had worked so hard on, from behavior to providing closure in my lessons, seemed to come together at once.

FIRST-GRADE TEACHER

Being able to sit down, not say a word, and watch the kids do it all themselves: the routines, the activities, the learning . . . the cleanup!

LANGUAGE ARTS TEACHER

Calling all 235 students in my school by name.

RELIGION TEACHER

Developing and implementing an effective behavior management program.

SPECIAL EDUCATION TEACHER

Everyone in the room actively engaged in a single project. We were like one big humming machine.

SECOND-GRADE TEACHER

Figuring out that I really do love teaching!

ALTERNATIVE EDUCATION TEACHER

Getting the children to respect and trust me.

READING TEACHER

Hearing that the children looked forward to coming to class and groaned when the day was over.

THIRD-GRADE TEACHER

It was nice to be excited to come back from the December vacation!

FIRST-GRADE TEACHER

Juggling all that teaching entails is something I was quite proud of.

SCIENCE TEACHER

Knowing that my after-school help was making a difference. Not only did the kids want to learn more about the subject, they liked spending time with me.

MATHEMATICS TEACHER

Leaving at the end of the day without having overdosed on coffee!

THIRD-GRADE TEACHER

Making the most of my strengths and coping with my weaknesses until they themselves became strengths.

GEOGRAPHY TEACHER

Not quitting was my greatest accomplishment that first year!

MUSIC TEACHER

Occasionally letting myself laugh felt good. And I found that the more confidence I had in my teaching, the less I had to worry about being a disciplinarian and the more I could enjoy the kids.

FOURTH-GRADE TEACHER

Perfect attendance. I just wanted to be with my students every day and to give them as much as I could.

SPECIAL EDUCATION TEACHER

Quickly and quietly getting my students down to work. I had put so much effort into establishing routines and here they were, mid-September, doing it automatically!

THIRD-GRADE TEACHER

Reading my first evaluation, accepting that I still needed improvement, and celebrating all that was going well.

GLOBAL STUDIES TEACHER

Surviving with my sense of humor intact!

SPANISH AND DRAMA TEACHER

Teaching a dyslexic fourth grader how to read.

MIDDLE SCHOOL PRINCIPAL

Uplifting feedback from a parent who had previously hated, or at least seemed to hate, everything I did with her child!

SECOND-GRADE TEACHER

Visualizing what my class would look like when in full swing and making it a reality. What a feeling!

SOCIAL STUDIES TEACHER

Watching children become fluent lovers of reading was my greatest accomplishment.

READING TEACHER

Xeroxing less worksheets while creating more hands-on, student-centered activities.

ENGLISH TEACHER

Yelling less and explaining more was my greatest accomplishment. I'd learned that yelling only gave me a headache!

FIRST-GRADE TEACHER

Zeroing in on the curriculum goals made me feel good. I'd gotten over the initial hump of learning how the school worked and was really getting down to teaching and enjoying my students!

KINDERGARTEN TEACHER